RESPOND TO THE GATE

SCOTT HARDING

Respond to the Gate
Copyright © 2025 Scott Harding

All rights reserved. No part of this manuscript may be reproduced by any means without the written permission of the author except for short passages used in critical reviews.

251009 HQ

CONTENTS

Introduction vii

1. FROM THE TERMINAL TO THE TARMAC 1
   One-Way Ticket to Trouble 1
   Crash, Tumble, and Spew 2
   Landscaping Bypass 3
   Clock Cam Sting 5
   The Not-So-Great Escape 6
   Parking Lot Fame 7
   Helicopters and Han Solo 7
   Cash in the Socks 8
   Special Delivery 9
   The Friend Who Didn't Exist 10
   Hearts on Her Hand 11
   Birthday Blues and Breath Tests 13
   The Cell Phone Standoff 14

2. EMERGENCIES ON THE FLIGHT LINE 17
   Communicable Concern 17
   Successful CPRs 18
   Food Poisoned Landing 19
   Too Much Air, Literally 20
   The Burning Bobcat 21
   The Final Boarding 22
   No Brakes! 23
   The Fatal Foggy Flight 24
   The Spider Bite That Wasn't 25
   Fentanyl in the Fleet Lot 26
   A Sudden Shift in the Situation 27

3. CRIMES OF DECEPTION — 29
- The Prepaid Card Caper — 29
- Forty Bucks for an iPhone — 30
- The Counterfeit Couple — 31
- Labor Day Cash-Out — 32
- The Scanner Scam — 33
- The Cross-Country Rental Car Con — 35
- The Washed Check Caper — 37
- Fraud in the Gold Booth — 38
- Contracts? Who Needs Contracts? — 39
- Faking The Stub — 40
- The $30,000 Lesson — 41
- Cash, Credit, and a Quick Hand — 42
- Plastic Crimes at the Pump — 43
- Plastic Lies on the Interstate — 45
- The Sky-High Scam — 46
- Selfies, Scams, and Stolen Rides — 47
- Strike Three, You're Out of Rentals — 48
- The Armenian Skimmer Crew — 49
- The LLC Hustlers — 50

4. ENGINES, EVASION, AND ARRESTS — 53
- The Hellcat Hustle — 54
- The Rogue Ride and Bumper Lock — 56
- Mustang to Mexico — 57
- The Walk-On Car Thief — 58
- From the State Park to the State Line — 60
- The Test Drive That Never Came Back — 60
- Campus Getaway — 61
- Dysfunctional Duo — 62
- Grand Theft: Exotic Edition — 64
- Camaro, Credit Cards, and the Dairy Queen Stakeout — 65
- The Rental Dukes of Hazzard — 67

5. FROM RINGS TO RUNWAYS — 69
- Felony Lane Intercept — 69
- Coast-to-Coast Pickpockets — 71

Closing the Lane	72
The Rabbit Bedding Traffickers	74
Felony Lane Training Day	75
The Ugly Shoes Case	76
Plea Deal Disgrace	78
Grindr Gotcha	80
Flight Risk Turned Felon Trail	82
6. INSIDE JOBS	**85**
Clocking In, Driving Out	85
The Midnight Fill-Ups	86
The Battery Bandit	87
The Vending Machine Caper	89
Fifty-One Dollars and a Lost Career	90
When the Gatekeeper Goes Rogue	91
Broken System, Broken Kids	93
The Phone, the Cash, and the Cleaning Lady Who Wouldn't Stay Quiet	94
61 Wives and 81 Kids	95
The Circuit Tracer Trail	97
Cashier's Cut: Parking Booth Embezzlement	98
The Restaurant Manager Who Cooked the Books	100
The Job Interview That Gave Him Away	101
Gas and GameStop	102
The Day Labor Dilemma	103
7. BAGS, SCAMS, AND STICKY FINGERS	**105**
The Duty-Free Counselor	105
The Jaguar Luggage Thief	106
The Purple Polka-Dot Bust	108
The Thanksgiving Baggage Crew	109
The Backpack Full of Keys	110
The Vanished Amazon Pallet	114
The Bikini Bait Phone	115
The Security Vest Heist	116
Like Mother, Like Daughter	118
The Firefighter Faker	119

Bra Money and a Bathroom Bust	120
The Student Who Studied Cars	122
No Free Parking	123
8. FALSE ALARMS, REAL CONSEQUENCES	125
The Drunken Threat	125
The Bear Spray Blowup	126
The Fraternity Fallout	128
The Disgruntled Attendant	129
Jealousy in the Air	130
9. REFLECTION	133

INTRODUCTION

Airports are small cities with hard deadlines. Most folks only ever see the concourses and coffee lines. I worked behind the curtain—at a public safety department where every officer is trained for police, fire, and EMS. One minute you're directing a lost family to baggage claim; the next you're suiting up for a fuel ramp fire, a medical call, or a threat that turns an airplane around at 30,000 feet.

I didn't start out chasing this life. I went to college planning to fly airplanes, took a few lessons, and realized the cockpit didn't click for me the way emergency work did. Criminal justice did. So did EMS. I earned my EMT license, joined the airport's Department of Public Safety, and climbed fast—Field Training Officer within two years, sergeant in under four. Over the next two decades I handled the "airport stuff" you've probably seen on TV—drunk passengers, lost luggage, gate disputes—and a lot of things you haven't: high-dollar retail crews moving through on weekend mileage runs, rental-fleet fraud that turns into interstate pursuits, covert stings on baggage belts, and the kind of medical calls that test whether training beats panic.

I started in February 2002, just months after 9/11. Back then, people were kinder—thankful to soldiers, cops, and brand new TSA screeners. Flights were fewer, tempers cooler. Today, terminals are packed, schedules stacked, nerves frayed, and by midmorning a shift can feel like walking into a live episode of Jerry Springer. Our officers roam the curbs and garages, patrol the airfield, work wrecks, haul prisoners, and partner with FBI, DEA, Secret Service, and Homeland Security. When the tone drops for a fire, we swap uniforms and roll. Later in my career, I was promoted to lieutenant and tasked with leading a growing criminal investigations division with three narcotic K-9 handlers and two other detectives.

These stories aren't theory. They are the cases and calls that stuck: a guidance counselor with million-miler confidence and a jacket full of stolen duty-free goods, a runaway saved in the nick of time, a "bear spray" evacuation that shut down a concourse, a skimmer crew undone by a rented plate and a bad weekend, the CPR saves we still talk about—and the ones we don't. They're about what goes wrong when thousands of strangers, tight timelines, and human nature meet in one building—and what it takes to keep that building safe.

Welcome to the part of the airport you never see.

FROM THE TERMINAL TO THE TARMAC

ONE-WAY TICKET TO TROUBLE

I WAS CALLED TO THE GATE TO SPEAK WITH AN AIRLINE operations supervisor about a possible juvenile runaway headed for Oakland, California. By the time I arrived, airline staff had already coaxed her off the plane. She looked calm enough, but you could tell she wasn't thrilled to see a uniformed officer waiting for her. As I walked her to our office, my sergeant came over the radio. Detroit Police had confirmed what we suspected—she was a reported runaway from their city. They wanted her detained and sent back home. Having kids of my own, I couldn't help but think of them. The thought of one of them being coaxed into running or feeling upset enough to buy a plane ticket and leave the state was hard to wrap my head around. This girl was so young. I kept the conversation light with her. She told me her family was in California and rattled off a phone number. But when my sergeant called, the man who answered refused to give his name and claimed he didn't know her. That was the crack in her story. A quick follow-up with her parents in Detroit confirmed the truth: she had left home without their knowledge. We made arrangements for her to board another flight where her parents would be waiting for her arrival. Walking her back toward the gate, I couldn't shake the thought—if she had made it all the way to California, the odds of her family ever seeing her again would have been slim. Sometimes the right intervention comes just in time. Any calls involving kids hit close to home for me, and this one stayed with me long after the paperwork was done.

CRASH, TUMBLE, AND SPEW

I was on patrol one summer night when I was dispatched to a hit-and-run near the terminal—possibly an impaired driver. I didn't have to go far. A red Chevrolet Cavalier sat in front of the service tunnel like it had finally given up. As I walked up, the driver stumbled out. He swayed like he was standing on a ship's deck, and the smell of alcohol hit me before he said a word. The windshield was shattered, both passenger-side tires were blown, and the inside looked like the recycling bin at a tailgate—eighteen open beer cans by my count. We had some concrete barriers in place because of construction, and it looked like he'd run the side of his car down most of them. A witness told us he had nearly run over three people before that. He failed the field sobriety tests miserably, and the breath test turned into a circus. Instead of blowing, he kept spitting into the tube like it was a game. I finally decided a hospital blood draw was our best bet. He didn't like that idea either. Before we even got into my car, he head-butted the trunk hard enough to leave a dent. Once inside, he vomited all over the back seat. At the hospital, he cursed at the nurse and refused to cooperate. By the end of the night, he was booked for DUI, open container, leaving the scene, vandalism, aggravated assault, and an implied consent violation. He managed to vomit two more times during booking. It was exactly the kind of night that reminded me why we'd replaced our cloth patrol car seats with hard plastic. Even with plastic, you can hose them out all you want, but the smell doesn't go away easily. Even worse if you're a sympathetic puker—and I'll admit, I am. Out of all the DUIs I worked over the years, this one stood out because of the sheer chaos. It wasn't just the mess he left behind; it was how close he came to killing someone before he finally lost control.

LANDSCAPING BYPASS

Some people will do just about anything to dodge a parking bill. As a patrol officer and a detective, I had to deal with many calls involving people who skipped out on airport parking, or at least tried to. I know airport parking rates have steadily climbed over the years, but theft is theft. One thing I appreciated was that airport operations and the parking management company would sometimes help people out and allow them to leave with a promissory note. It was a case-by-case basis, and they didn't do it often, but to those that truly needed the help in exigent circumstances, they gave it to them. One afternoon, I got dispatched to a call about a truck that had plowed straight through the landscaping near the long-term lot and disappeared toward the interstate. When I got there, the scene looked like a small tornado had touched down—broken branches, flattened bushes, and deep tire tracks cutting a brand-new "exit" through the carefully manicured greenery by the flagpoles. A transit supervisor on scene told me he'd watched an older-model red pickup—maybe a GMC or Chevy—blast through the landscaping and slip out onto a discreet service road headed west toward the interstate. I swept the highway as far as the next exit down but never saw him. Maintenance was already figuring out how much it would cost to repair the damage, and from the looks of it, the bill wouldn't be small. Not long after, the driver called the airport operations center. He admitted he was the one who'd done it and even explained why: he didn't have the money to pay his $178 parking bill, so he figured driving through the bushes was a better option. Video from the parking booth confirmed it. Just before his landscaping escape, the parking attendant had told him to go park his truck back in the lot until he could pay. Instead, he took what I can only describe as the "express lane" through our flowerbeds. A quick check on his information revealed his license was suspended, he had an outstanding local warrant, and the Florida address he gave didn't even exist on Google Maps. The damage estimate was already pushing $500—and that didn't include the parking fee he was trying to avoid. Some people drive out of the airport. This guy crashed his way out. It cost him a charge of felony vandalism and leaving the scene of an accident involving property damage.

CLOCK CAM STING

Some calls don't start with alarms or radio traffic—they start with a quiet complaint and a suspicion. One week near Christmas, I got one of those calls from a commercial building on airport property. The building housed several businesses, including a personnel management company, and one of their holiday traditions was giving each employee an envelope of cash to donate to a charity of their choice. That year, a couple of those envelopes vanished right out of people's desks. Management wanted answers, so I set a trap. Near the airport was a regional organized crime information center that had a technical division. If there was something they could install a covert camera into, they had it in this room. When I walked in there, I felt like James Bond hitting up "Q" for new tech. Energy drink cans, fake fire alarm panels, wall clocks, electric pole transformers; anything a camera could fit in, they had it. I decided on a desk-mounted alarm clock—the kind that blends in with office décor. I planted a fresh envelope of cash in the office, and it didn't take long. The envelope went missing again. When we reviewed the footage from the alarm clock camera, the culprit wasn't a coworker at all. She was a member of the cleaning staff. We brought her in, showed her the evidence, and she admitted to taking the money. She told us she had several children and was just trying to make ends meet. She barely made minimum wage. I issued her a citation and let her go. It wasn't the case you celebrate, but the office management was happy with the quick resolution—and the fact that their holiday tradition could continue without someone dipping into the donations.

THE NOT-SO-GREAT ESCAPE

I received a call from one of the metro detectives who was trying to catch up to a suspect that had allegedly taken a white Honda Civic without permission. Inside the car were a credit card, more than a thousand dollars in cash, and the vehicle owner's ID. The detective had information that the guy was headed to the airport to catch a flight out of town. My team and I started searching. It didn't take long—he'd already checked in for his flight and was browsing in a concourse store like he didn't have a care in the world. When we approached, he admitted he'd driven the Civic to the airport and even pulled the key from his pocket to prove it. He walked us to the short-term garage where the car was parked. While we were there, he pointed out the base of a concrete column where he'd ditched the keychain. By then, the car's owner had made it clear she wanted him prosecuted for theft, so the cuffs went on. When I asked about the cash, he said he'd used a few hundred to buy his ticket. The rest? "In my sock," he said. Sure enough, there was $800 tucked inside, and another $120 in his shorts pocket. The vehicle was recovered, the money returned, and the airline refunded the cost of the ticket. His trip was still going to involve travel—just not the kind he'd planned, and definitely not in first class. What always struck me about this case was how calm he was—checked in, shopping, not a care in the world. Some criminals act guilty; others act as if they'll never get caught.

PARKING LOT FAME

I got a call from the parking management company about a vehicle that had skipped out on parking fees. It wasn't the first time someone had tried to dodge payment, but this case had a twist: the couple responsible had posted a video of it on social media. In the video, the female passenger filmed her boyfriend driving out of the garage without paying, giving step-by-step instructions on how to do it. What they didn't realize was that the video showed the vehicle's license plate they followed out of the garage—along with a visible date and time stamp. I reviewed airport surveillance and was able to match the video details with our footage, which gave me everything I needed. I identified the car, confirmed the license plate, and got a warrant for the driver on a theft of services charge. I also emailed him, advising him to turn himself in. Shortly after, the girlfriend called and offered to pay for the parking. She was told that restitution could be taken care of as part of a plea deal in court. Surprisingly, many of the comments on their social media video were actually in support of the airport, mercilessly bashing her and her boyfriend for skipping out on parking—which was refreshing to see for a change.

HELICOPTERS AND HAN SOLO

As airport police officers, we were often called on to assist with VIP details—everything from presidential visits to celebrity escorts. Over the years, I had the chance to meet former vice presidents, first ladies, and even exchange a quick hello with a former British prime minister. Some of the more memorable encounters came from escorting celebrities to and from their flights. I provided security for folks like Miley Cyrus, Billy Bob Thornton, and Kevin Costner. Most of the celebrities I did interact with were polite and approachable—often signing autographs for fans who recognized them. There were a few who weren't so gracious, but I won't name names. I've been a fan of many of them, but I never really got starstruck. Well—almost never. One day, a helicopter landed on the field with two pilots aboard. I didn't think much of it at first, but as I watched them prep for departure, it hit me: the pilot was Harrison Ford. By the time I realized it, they were already finishing their pre-flight checks and climbing back in. As a lifelong Star Wars fan, missing the chance to speak with Han Solo himself was a definite letdown. One of the coolest moments during my career didn't involve a politician or a movie star. It came from a commercial airline pilot who moonlighted flying helicopters. He was landing as I pulled up in my patrol car. After shutting down, he motioned for me to come over, opened the door, and casually asked, "Want to take a quick spin?" Of course, I said yes. We flew for about ten minutes over a nearby lake, just chatting and enjoying the view. It wasn't official, it wasn't planned—but it was unforgettable.

CASH IN THE SOCKS

Rental car management called one afternoon with a problem—a customer had left seven envelopes of cash inside a vehicle, and when they were turned in, some of the money was missing. About $1,700 short. Video surveillance quickly told the story. One employee cleaning the car found the envelopes, then walked them over to another employee working nearby. The two had a brief conversation, tucked the envelopes into another vehicle, and later slipped into the break room. Odd behavior, considering the rule was crystal clear: anything found in a rental car went straight to a supervisor, no exceptions. Both employees denied wrongdoing when questioned. One pointed to the other, saying he still had the cash. The second swore he didn't. But the footage was enough for probable cause, and both were arrested and transported to the city jail. That's where the real kicker came. During booking, correctional officers called me over—they'd just found $1,710 stuffed into the suspect's socks, split between both feet. Apparently, he thought his shoes were as good as a bank vault. The cash was seized as evidence, and the customer was told it would eventually be returned after the case made its way through court. These were a couple of guys who had steady jobs, paychecks they could count on, and a clear policy to follow. All it took was a few envelopes of cash to throw it all away.

SPECIAL DELIVERY

The call came from Metro's Crime Suppression Unit—they'd stumbled onto something in the middle of a surveillance operation. They were sitting on a parking lot close to the airport, watching for drug activity, when a black Chevy rolled in and parked. Nothing unusual at first. Then another car pulled up beside it. The driver of the

Chevy popped his trunk, hauled out a big black trash bag, and dropped it into the other car's trunk. The handoff was quick and quiet, but it was suspicious enough for Metro to follow up. A traffic stop on the second vehicle revealed the truth. Inside the trash bag weren't drugs but dozens of packages—each stuffed with cell phones. Not new ones, either. These were broken phones packaged for shipment, the kind that normally head off to repair facilities before being recycled back into circulation. The haul was worth over $10,000. The driver of the second car, a parolee, gave up the story right away: the man in the black Chevy worked at the post office facility on airport property. He'd been looking for certain marked packages that contained damaged cell phones, slipping them out of the building, and selling them off with help from his partner. I contacted the post office's own investigator, and the employee didn't get far. He was arrested on state charges for theft over $10,000. What started as a routine drug surveillance ended up taking down a postal worker running a side hustle that could have put a real dent in the supply chain. I have no idea how long he had been stealing those phones, but they were in unique packages, which made it easy for him to spot. If you sent your cell phone off for repair in one of those first-class brown envelopes and it never made it, check with these guys.

THE FRIEND WHO DIDN'T EXIST

Rental companies don't just lose track of cars by accident—when a vehicle goes missing, there's usually a trail. Here, it led straight back to one of their own employees. A manager called to report a grey Honda CRV that had been missing from inventory since the fall. Months later, the vehicle mysteriously reappeared on airport cameras, pulling into the garage—not once, but twice—picking up the same employee. When questioned, she admitted her own personal car had broken down about the same time the CRV vanished. But rather than come clean, she pointed the finger at a supposed "best friend" named Hope. The problem? She had no phone number, no address—just a Snapchat handle. When pressed to call this "Hope," her phone lit up with missed calls she refused to answer. Under pressure, she finally dialed. A woman answered, claimed she'd abandoned the rental on the side of the road, then promptly hung up when asked about a report. The Snapchat profile didn't even say "Hope." It was all smoke and mirrors. Her story crumbled with every question. She couldn't explain who had the vehicle or where it was. The company pressed charges, and she was arrested on the spot for theft over $10,000. The following day, Metro located the Honda—abandoned on a side street and towed to impound. In the end, the cover-up was almost worse than the theft. The car was found, but the "friend" was just a story she couldn't keep straight.

HEARTS ON HER HAND

In early 2019, car rental management contacted me regarding yet another stolen rental vehicle. According to the manager, a female had walked up to their counter on New Year's Eve and rented a car using a Wisconsin driver's license in the name of J⎯⎯ R⎯⎯. The agreement said the vehicle was due back January 4th at noon. By mid-January, it still hadn't returned. Digging deeper, the manager learned the credit card the female used was fraudulent—issued by a bank out of Australia—and the driver's license number on the contract wasn't valid either. The scam was pretty straightforward: counterfeit ID, stolen credit card, walk away with a brand-new rental. The problem was, by the time the fraud surfaced, JR was long gone. The rental manager asked us to report the vehicle stolen, and it was entered into NCIC. While searching a criminal justice database, I found a JR out of Wisconsin who had a record of prior arrests. The license number didn't match what was on the rental contract, but one detail stood out—she had a tattoo on her right hand with hearts and the name *Jasmine*. The photos the car rental manager had pulled from their counter matched that description perfectly. Once the vehicle was flagged in NCIC, we got a delayed hit from Cook County, Georgia. A deputy had just pulled the car over for speeding. JR was behind the wheel. That was the break we needed to positively identify her. The trail didn't end in Georgia, though. The very next day, the car turned up in Miami, Florida, and JR was arrested again, this time with another passenger. Miami detectives said the car was loaded with counterfeit currency when it was stopped. What started as a single overdue rental had escalated into fraud, identity theft, and counterfeit money—stretching from Tennessee, through Georgia, all the way to South Florida. A tattoo on a hand connected the dots across three states. Even in the age of fake IDs and counterfeit cards, sometimes the truth shows up in plain sight. I chuckle every time I see someone in the news with many unmistakable tattoos. I have tattoos myself, but if you're pursuing a life of crime they will not help with your success.

BIRTHDAY BLUES AND BREATH TESTS

During my career, I was a DUI instructor and handled more than a few DUI arrests. One that stuck with me started when a car flew past my marked patrol unit one night at a high rate of speed. The driver—a local schoolteacher—clearly didn't realize who she'd just passed. She'd been downtown celebrating her birthday and, from the moment I spoke to her roadside, it was obvious she shouldn't be driving. I called for backup so another officer could sit with her vehicle while I moved her somewhere safer to run field sobriety tests. I always preferred a controlled environment—flat, well lit, out of the elements. At our department, that meant the firetruck bays back at the station. While we waited, her boyfriend climbed out of the passenger seat. He was a small guy, especially compared to her. I told him to wait in the car, but he stayed outside, trying to plead her case. "It's her birthday," he said. "Cut her a break." Before I could even ask him again to get back inside, she turned on him—loud, aggressive, and tearing into him right there in front of me and the arriving officer. I almost felt bad for the guy. In the end, she was arrested for DUI and became verbally abusive to everyone. She tried to play the "I'm a schoolteacher" card, but it didn't change a thing. At one point, I gave her a full-on lecture about the dangers of drinking and driving. It wasn't my usual style, but it worked—she finally stopped talking. I helped teach DUI investigations and field sobriety testing at the state police academy for several years. On the last day of training, we would invite people to come in and drink alcohol in a controlled environment, so the police recruits could practice administering the field sobriety tests and see how effective they are. We never had a shortage of volunteer drinkers for that training!

THE CELL PHONE STANDOFF

It started with a call to Gate C9—an aircraft that had just pushed back from the gate was now taxiing back in. The reason? A passenger refused to turn off her cell phone. That alone doesn't happen every day, so I knew there was more to the story. When I arrived, the airline supervisors filled me in. The passenger had been told twice to power down before takeoff. The second time, she'd fired back by calling the flight attendant a "bitch." That was enough for the crew to bring the plane back. Things didn't cool off when she deplaned. As she walked off, she threw another insult over her shoulder. That's when the flight attendant reportedly grabbed her from behind and whispered something in her ear. Depending on whom you asked, it was a few stern words... or something much more colorful. I spoke with the passenger, who admitted to the insult but insisted she'd complied with the phone request. She wanted to press charges for the grab. I explained the process—since I wasn't there to witness it, she'd have to go downtown to night court, tell her story to a judicial commissioner, and let him decide if there was enough evidence for a misdemeanor assault against the flight attendant. For a moment, she was ready to do it. Then she looked at the departure board, saw another flight to Dallas leaving soon, and decided the court date could wait. She took my card, said she understood, and hustled toward her new gate. By the time I cleared the area, the only things left were a delayed flight, a couple of bruised egos, and a reminder that even something as small as a phone left on can blow up into a full-blown incident.

EMERGENCIES ON THE FLIGHT LINE

COMMUNICABLE CONCERN

It was at the height of the SARS scare, and the entire airport felt like it was holding its breath. For those not old enough to remember, the SARS and Avian flu scares came long before COVID. Any call about sick passengers could turn into something serious, and when operations radioed about a flight inbound from Mexico with several people reportedly ill, my stomach tightened. I was part of the department's Hazardous Materials Team, so I had more training than the others working that day. We met the aircraft at the gate, masks on, and kept the jet bridge clear. No one got off until we'd spoken to the sick passengers first. Three of them told me they'd all eaten at the same Burger King in the Cancun airport just before boarding. The fourth had been sick for two days already and hadn't eaten with the others. They all had the same symptoms—nausea and vomiting—but no cough, no fever. After a quick check with Customs, we cleared the rest of the passengers to deplane. The sick travelers got a secondary medical check, and none of them wanted to be transported to a hospital. Back then, with global headlines running on fear, we had to treat every case like it might be the real thing. Thankfully, this one was just bad airport food, not the start of a local health crisis. We had to speak with city and state health officials before clearing the scene and asked the affected passengers to follow up with their doctors. I had a hand in writing our agency's first communicable disease policy—what started as a plan for the avian flu scare, then SARS, and eventually became a general "communicable disease" policy. As part of the Hazardous Materials Team, I had all the protective gear we might need, but respiratory masks on a plane will stop passengers in their tracks. I'll never forget their expressions—wide-eyed, frozen—like deer caught in the landing lights.

SUCCESSFUL CPRS

Over the years, I responded to more CPR calls than I can count. We'd installed dozens of AEDs throughout the terminal, and by the time I stepped down as the department's EMS Director, the airport had a 50% survival rate for sudden cardiac arrest. The national average was 16%. That success wasn't luck—it resulted from preparation. We trained a high percentage of our officers, encouraged bystander involvement, and made sure AEDs were never far away. The formula was simple: recognize cardiac arrest quickly, start CPR immediately, and apply an AED as soon as possible. At the airport, those steps often happened within seconds, and AED use was usually within minutes.

In several cases, we were so fast that by the time the ambulance arrived, the person was not only resuscitated but awake and talking. Other times, it didn't matter how quickly we moved—their condition or injuries were simply too severe. One of the most striking things was watching the surveillance footage afterward. You'd see a person standing or walking in the terminal collapse, and almost instantly, bystanders, employees, and responders would spring into action. The airport rarely released those videos, but they were a reminder that in moments like that, people's best instincts come forward. In today's climate, I wish we saw more of that. I was a CPR and Emergency Medical Responder (EMR) instructor for many years. It was gratifying to hear stories of people I had trained who had helped save the lives of others. Not just those in public safety or medical fields, but others who I had certified in CPR and the use of an AED. It's easy training, and I encourage everyone to go through it. They now have online courses to get certified.

FOOD POISONED LANDING

I was in charge one weekend as Shift Commander when the Air Traffic Control Tower rang down with a message that got my full attention: the pilot of a small aircraft was experiencing severe stomach pain and wasn't sure he could land. I rolled with the airport crash trucks to the runway, scanning for the incoming aircraft. Fortunately, he managed to touch down without incident and taxied quickly to the parking ramp. When we pulled up, he had already shut the aircraft down but was still sitting in the pilot's seat—the only person onboard. Climbing inside, I could see he was in agony. His feet and hands were clenched, and he said there was no way he could get out of the seat on his own. We called a mechanic and removed two other seats to make room. When the ambulance arrived, it took several of us to lift him from the front seat onto a backboard. From there, we carefully worked him out of the aircraft. If this was food poisoning, it was the worst I'd ever seen. This man literally could not move. I was just glad he'd had enough left in him to safely land that airplane—a twin-turboprop, high-wing Mitsubishi. Not exactly the plane you want to be flying when you can barely stay conscious, and certainly not for someone without many hours in the logbook.

TOO MUCH AIR, LITERALLY

By the time I joined the department, I was already an experienced EMT. Medical calls were a big part of the job—over 30% of the total calls in the terminal were medical-related. With more than a million people traveling through every month, something was bound to happen. About a third of our department held EMT licenses, and the rest were EMR. I taught the EMR program in-house, making sure everyone was ready when things went bad. Some officers loved the police work and hated medical calls. Others enjoyed firefighting and weren't crazy about arrests. But at our department, you did it all—whether you liked it or not. One midnight shift, I got a call that was as preventable as it was ugly. An aircraft maintenance worker skipped most of the rules in his safety manual and filled an aircraft tire while it was sitting on the bed of his pickup truck. He overfilled it. The tire exploded. The main blast missed his head by inches, but caught his hand and arm. His humerus bone snapped, and parts of his hand were scattered across the ramp. We splinted his arm, wrapped his hand to control the bleeding, and got him en route to the hospital. When he arrived, the surgeons made an unusual request—they wanted us to collect as much of the hand as we could from the ramp so they could try to reconstruct it. We went back, picked up what we could, and brought it to them. Through it all, he stayed calm—calmer than most people would have been in his situation. It was a preventable accident, and it could have been a fatal one. Fortunately, he survived without life-threatening injuries.

THE BURNING BOBCAT

One Saturday night, I was serving as Commander when the control tower reported an active fire on the west side of the airfield at the cargo ramp. I rolled out with the crash trucks, and even from across the airfield I could see the smoke, glowing orange in the ramp lights. When we arrived, the source became apparent—a pickup truck, the kind we called a bobcat, had caught fire after its engine overheated. The driver had already walked away, not realizing what was coming next. Flames spread fast, jumping from the bobcat to two nearby tugs. One of those tugs had handheld fuel canisters sitting on top, which added a layer of danger we didn't need. Our smallest fire truck, an F-550, hit the visible flames first with water from its bumper turret. The larger crash truck backed it up, using its roof turret for extra suppression. Even after it looked like the fire was out, heavy smoke still poured from under the bobcat's hood. I told the firefighters to get into their bunker gear, pull a hose line, and pop the hood. Once they did, they knocked out what was left of the engine fire. Thankfully, no aircraft were parked on the cargo ramp that night, so the damage stayed minimal. We'd seen our share of ground equipment fires over the years, and with the right apparatus, they were usually quick work. The bigger concern was always the same—chemical runoff into the terminal ramp drainage systems. Fortunately, our airport had a safeguard: a system to shut down the spillways leaving the property in case of hazardous runoff. That night, the system stayed on standby—no harm to the environment, and another fire put in the "handled" column.

THE FINAL BOARDING

An airline supervisor called into dispatch requesting medical help. The situation didn't sound routine. A gate agent had flagged him down about the condition of a man in a wheelchair, and when the supervisor arrived, the man was slumped over to one side, drool running from his mouth. He wasn't responding to anyone. His daughter was there and told the supervisor her father was heavily medicated, and she was just trying to get him back home. The supervisor wasn't buying it. He called for medical assistance right away. The first officer on the scene was Tom. Tom was a good guy and an outstanding cop, but he'd earned the nickname "The Reaper"—not because of any bad luck on his part, but because of the sheer number of medical calls he'd handled over his career where someone didn't make it. Tom was slow and methodical. If he ever got rattled, you couldn't tell. At the gate, he checked the man's pulse, then told the airline supervisor to help him lift the man from the wheelchair so they could start CPR. The supervisor froze like a deer in headlights. Tom called out "CPR in progress" over the radio. I arrived as the second officer on scene and started setting up the AED while Tom continued compressions. The AED wouldn't advise a shock, and after several minutes, city EMS took over. The man didn't make it. We weren't sure exactly when he had passed. My gut told me the daughter knew her father's time was close and was just trying to get him home, maybe because they didn't have the money or means to do it any other way. Sadly, he never made it back.

NO BRAKES!

Back when the rental cars were still housed underneath the terminal, I was dispatched to a wreck in the area. When I got there, it looked like a demolition derby gone wrong. The vehicle in question had plowed into several parked cars, and the windshield had a hole in it big enough to put an arm through. Behind the wheel sat an older woman, her arm bleeding heavily, with blood dripping down onto the pavement. She explained what happened: she'd gotten into the car, put it in drive, and accidentally hit the gas to move forward not backward. Instead of correcting herself and hitting the brake, she panicked and pressed the accelerator even harder. Holding the wheel in a death grip, she'd spun the car in a wide circle, smashing into multiple vehicles. At some point in the chaos, her elbow went through the windshield, leaving a nasty gash. I wrapped the wound to slow the bleeding until the ambulance arrived. She was polite, clearly embarrassed, and—

thankfully—the only person injured. Had anyone been walking nearby, the scene could've turned tragic fast. Incidents like this are why most states allow law enforcement or family members to request a driver re-evaluation for elderly motorists. It's never a simple conversation, but it's about protecting both the driver and everyone around them. In her case, the injury wasn't life-threatening. Her pride, though, might've taken the bigger hit.

THE FATAL FOGGY FLIGHT

One of the toughest crash scenes I ever experienced started in the thickest fog I'd seen in over forty years of living in a southern state. It was early morning, and you could barely see more than a few feet ahead. The pilot of a small Cessna had been circling a smaller airport during the night before heading to our larger one. He never radioed the tower. Instead, he came in steep, trying to line up with a runway. By the time he broke through the fog, he was too low. He bounced across the runway, cartwheeled, and the aircraft burst into flames. Some smaller planes don't have instruments capable of landing in those conditions. Even if they do, the pilot must be certified to fly using instruments only. With the kind of fog blanketing the airfield that morning, there was no way he could see the runway—and no avionics to guide him down. The wreckage burned through the night, coming to rest in the grass between the runway and taxiway. Around 10 a.m., a commercial airline pilot noticed debris and told the tower to have airport operations clear it away. Nobody realized it was from a small plane crash. When an ops agent rolled up, they found the wreckage and called for help. The crash trucks responded, but the heavy fog slowed them down. What they found was a cold, burned-out fuselage with the pilot still inside. My team, along with federal investigators, set up a perimeter and began mapping the scene. We later learned the pilot had flown in from Canada, and his route wasn't part of the original flight plan. We suspected he was trying to leave the country to evade charges back home. In an odd twist, he'd listed a very famous country music singer as his next of kin—with no relation whatsoever.

THE SPIDER BITE THAT WASN'T

As an EMT, I handled my fair share of medical calls, especially back in my patrol days. One of the funniest ones started when a woman approached me in the terminal, clearly worked up. She told me she had a fear of spiders—and thought she had been bitten. She turned around and pointed to a small spot on the back of her white shirt where blood had seeped through. It stood out right away. Growing up in the South, I knew most spiders have enough bite force to break skin, but I also knew they're not usually neat about it. I told her I'd look, and we walked down to the small medical office in the terminal. When she lifted the back of her shirt, I diagnosed it instantly—not a bite, just a large pimple that had popped. A couple more were nearby. I explained the situation as respectfully as I could, but she was thoroughly embarrassed. I told her not to be—these things happen more often than people think. She went on her way to catch her flight, probably avoiding the insect section of the gift shop. I've actually only dealt with one real spider bite in my EMT career. That case came from another woman, already treated at the hospital, who asked if I could change the dressing on her leg before her flight. A brown recluse had bitten her—and if you don't know about those, the venom destroys living tissue. Thankfully, she'd gone to the hospital right after the bite and was treated with heavy antibiotics. The recluse bite can be severe if not treated. When I peeled back the bandage, it was bad. I've worked on plenty of trauma scenes involving car crashes, but rotting flesh is never a pleasant sight. I changed the dressing, sealed the old one in the biohazard container, and made sure she was good to go.

FENTANYL IN THE FLEET LOT

For years, drugs had been a problem at the airport, but it wasn't until heroin and fentanyl started showing up that we began seeing overdoses. And when they hit, they hit hard. The call came in from the rental car lot—two employees had gone missing during their shift. A co-worker went looking and found them slumped over in a pickup truck. Neither was conscious. We rolled up fast. Narcan was administered to both. One came back. The other didn't. He was a husband and father, and losing him was gut-wrenching. As the investigation unfolded, we learned he'd found drugs in a rental car that had been towed back to the lot. Thinking it was cocaine, he called over another employee to try it with him. They didn't know it was laced with fentanyl until it was too late. The survivor told us from his hospital bed that the moment he snorted it, he knew something wasn't right. Seconds later, he was out cold. There was no dealer to track down, no suspect to chase. That's what makes fentanyl so dangerous

—it's not just the pills. It's the fact that so many street drugs are laced with it now, and no one knows exactly what they're putting in their system. The dealers don't even know what they're selling. We'd already had cars pull into the airport with passengers overdosing inside. Every sworn officer carried Narcan, and we used it more than once. This wasn't the first fatal overdose at the airport. And sadly, I doubt it will be the last. What stuck with me was how powerless it felt. We had Narcan, training, experience—but sometimes even that isn't enough. Watching a father's life end in a parking lot because of one poor decision made the fentanyl crisis feel closer, sharper, and more personal. Several members of our division were federally sworn with the DEA, and one is probably one of the best drug investigators in the country. It takes a lot to work dope investigations full-time, but they're getting a lot of poison off the streets and putting some serious dealers in prison for life. And I'm grateful to have worked alongside them.

A SUDDEN SHIFT IN THE SITUATION

I was the shift commander one weekend when a call came out about a security guard possibly having a heart attack. I arrived quickly and found him lying on the ground—awake and alert, but clearly in distress. After speaking with him, we learned that he had been dealing with significant constipation and had taken laxatives to get some relief. Unfortunately, as he was walking back to his work truck, the laxatives kicked in hard and fast. The sudden physical response overwhelmed him, and he'd briefly lost consciousness. By the time he came to, things had gotten messy—literally. EMS arrived and transported him to the hospital for evaluation. Thankfully, he was released a short time later with no lasting issues. What stuck with me about this call was how quickly it shifted. We responded thinking we had a heart attack on our hands, only to discover it was an over-the-counter medication gone wrong. It was a reminder that in emergency response, you treat what you see, not what you expect—and sometimes even the "routine" medical calls come with surprises you don't forget.

CRIMES OF DECEPTION

THE PREPAID CARD CAPER

AIRLINE MANAGERS CALLED ME ONE AFTERNOON WITH A theft report that was clever in its simplicity. An international passenger owed about $600 in baggage fees but only had cash. Since the airline doesn't take cash directly, she was sent to a kiosk to load the money onto a prepaid Visa card. An employee at the ticket counter helped her through the process. So far, so good—until the employee waived all the baggage fees in the airline's system. The passenger boarded her flight without paying a dime, and the $600 prepaid card? That stayed in the employee's pocket. Hours later, the card resurfaced—used not for shopping or bills, but to pay for parking at the airport's long-term lot. When I reviewed the video footage from the exit lane, there was no doubt about who swiped it. What was supposed to be company revenue turned into a personal parking pass, and one employee's shortcut out of the lot ended up being her ticket straight into an investigation. The airline management dove further into their records and discovered the employee had done it on several other occasions. They prosecuted her, and she was arrested on several counts of theft.

FORTY BUCKS FOR AN IPHONE

Metro detectives called me about a theft report tied back to the airport—a newer Apple iPhone that had gone missing after a traveler returned his rental car. He'd accidentally left the phone inside, and by the time he realized it, the rental company couldn't find it. It didn't take long to trace. The phone had been fed into an ecoATM machine the very next day, traded for forty dollars cash. Those machines don't just take your device; they log everything—driver's license, photos, the works. You can typically find them at Walmarts and other retailers. It is a quick way to sell old electronic devices, although not for much money. When I pulled the transaction, the suspect's identity was right there in the database. She turned out to be a temporary contract worker who cleaned cars for the rental company. Oddly enough, management told me she hadn't even cleaned that vehicle. More likely, someone else passed her the phone, and she ran it through the machine for quick money. Either way, she was caught on camera at the kiosk, and that was enough for a warrant. EcoATM agreed to ship the phone back so it could be returned to its rightful owner. They were great to work with when stolen devices ended up in their machines. In the end, a thousand-dollar iPhone had been traded for the price of a tank of gas—and a set of criminal charges.

THE COUNTERFEIT COUPLE

I was investigating a stolen rental SUV. It started with a ping from OnStar—a Suburban belonging to Hertz had surfaced at a downtown hotel. When we got there with Metro detectives and Hertz reps, the SUV was sitting with the valet, stuffed full of new merchandise. Inside the driver's door were keys to two more rentals, both from Enterprise. It looked like someone had gone on a shopping spree. The auto theft guys asked the fraud unit to respond as well. The hotel room tied to the vehicle led us to a man using the name "Ryan." He denied renting the Suburban and tried to pin it on a friend, but the evidence didn't back him up. A search of the room turned up crystal meth, piles of merchandise, a laptop, printer, magnetic card encoder, and stacks of gift cards. It wasn't just a stolen car—it was a mobile fraud shop. The paper trail told the rest of the story. He'd been renting vehicles under a fake Texas driver's license, complete with a real license number but someone else's photo. The credit cards didn't belong to him either. Enterprise confirmed one of their Yukons was missing under the same fraudulent ID. Another vehicle tied to him was reported in Chicago. By the time the warrants were written, he was facing three counts of auto theft—two from Hertz, one from Enterprise—on top of the fraud and drug evidence sitting in his hotel room. Ironically, the story didn't end there. Just a few months later, we were investigating another rental car theft—this time involving a woman. A neighboring police department was onto her for using a stolen credit card at a pharmacy. She made one small mistake at checkout: she typed in her mother's cell phone number to get the reward points.

Surveillance video showed her climbing into a rental car that traced back to the airport. Like before, it had been obtained with a counterfeit ID tied to a stolen identity. Turned out, she was his girlfriend—and he'd taught her the tricks of the trade. We monitored his jail calls, and he even hinted to her she was lucky she hadn't been caught yet. Her luck didn't last. Warrants were issued, and her part in the scheme caught up with her too. In the end, it wasn't just one fraudster running cars out of the airport—it was a team, and both of them wound up exactly where their hustle was bound to take them.

LABOR DAY CASH-OUT

One of the larger cyber cases I investigated involved a Romanian national who I caught dead to rights. On Labor Day weekend, a group email went out to several area investigators, both local and federal, involving a "cash-out" suspect. "Cash-out" is a bank term that means someone is using multiple stolen debit card numbers at one or two ATMs and making back-to-back cash withdrawals. Many of these suspects use rental cars to help facilitate their crimes. That's where I got involved. The bank investigator was one of the best I've ever worked with. She'd received an alarm on the ATM and was able to pull video footage of the suspect and the rear of the vehicle, including the license plate. I learned that the vehicle in question had been rented from my airport and was due back the morning the cash-outs were occurring, which happened to be Labor Day. I drove into work and set up surveillance at the entrance to the rental car garage. I was there for maybe 30 minutes before the vehicle came rolling up. I waited for the suspect to get out of the rental car and approached him in police gear. I placed him in handcuffs and explained why I was contacting him. Inside the satchel he was carrying was over $40k in cash and 100+ cloned debit cards with the PIN numbers written on them. He told me if I let him go, I could walk away with the cash. He only wished. I ran his name, and saw he had an outstanding federal warrant for ATM skimming out of New York totaling over $500k. He was interviewed by me and the USSS and was booked on more federal charges. The $40k and cloned cards were seized as evidence. A lengthy investigation ensued, and we discovered that a local retail pharmacy chain had recently installed self-checkout kiosks for their customers. The suspect and his wife entered a dozen of these pharmacies in August and placed skimmer overlays on the debit card machines. They left the overlays on them for almost a month and pulled them the weekend before Labor Day. They thought it was the perfect time. Once he pulled the debit card numbers from the overlay devices, he had over 100 cloned debit cards. Then he went to the ATMs to use them. Although I recovered $40k that day, he had taken out over $180k in less than 72 hours. He was ordered to pay it all back in federal court. His wife still has warrants, and we believe she fled the country once she learned I had arrested her husband.

THE SCANNER SCAM

One morning I received a call from a neighboring agency that was working on an investigation with a major grocery store chain. Corporate investigators with the grocery store advised that they had a suspect they had been trying to catch for months who was flying all over the country and stealing inventory scanners from their stores. Whenever you see an employee of a grocery or retailer scanning products, typically they're holding a handheld scanner that looks sort of like the ray-gun from Star Trek. This is basically a smartphone inside a case that they use for logging inventory. I learned these scanners could go from $500-$1000 each. Several came up missing in this neighboring jurisdiction, and the grocery store investigators believed the suspect was still in town. They had already identified him from previous thefts but always seemed to be a day behind his activities. I ran his name and, sure enough, he had flown into our airport and rented a car. The car was still outstanding, so we entered it into our LPR cameras to notify us when it returned. It wasn't long before we received the alert and headed over to the rental car garage. We arrested him on the warrants the neighboring agency had already sworn out against him. There were two inventory scanners in his luggage, but we knew there were more. I dug further into his luggage and found a receipt from FedEx, where he had just dropped off two boxes weighing 50 pounds. Bingo! We responded to FedEx and took possession of the boxes. After a search warrant was signed, we found that the boxes contained 100 scanners from the grocery stores and a couple of other retailers. He was attempting to ship them to a woman in Florida, who was then selling them overseas for a higher profit. Federal agents paid her a visit later that week. The grocery store chain didn't elaborate, but we estimated he had taken close to a million dollars' worth of these scanners over the better part of 18 months. His home was back in New

Jersey, but he never made the flight. This guy was going to be locked up for years, moving from jurisdiction to jurisdiction all over the US to answer to the same charges in those areas.

THE CROSS-COUNTRY RENTAL CAR CON

Car rental fraud is rampant in the US. We had our fair share of it for several years before we really began cracking down on suspects. The rental car companies started adding technology to help identify fake driver's licenses. They also began implementing internal software to help identify possible fraudulent online rental activity. One case I handled involved a guy traveling all over the US to rent cars from various airports. He was using counterfeit IDs and renting a couple of cars from different companies. He came to our airport, and the rental car investigator caught on to his activities. The investigator contacted me and advised that the suspect had picked up a car the day before using a fake ID with a stolen identity, and he was scheduled to do it again that day. The suspect came in and got a car unnoticed before the rental investigator realized he was there. A few minutes after he pulled out of the garage, the rental car investigator gave me the vehicle's location: a nearby gas station. Three of us drove to the location, and sure enough, he was sitting at a gas pump in the driver's seat and appeared to be looking at his phone. I pulled up behind the car, activated my blue lights, and walked up to the driver's side window. I already knew who he was and called him by his first name and told him to get out of the car. As I opened the door, he slammed the gas pedal and took off, straight out of the parking lot onto a four-lane road. How he didn't get hit, I'll never know. Our pursuit policy does not allow us to chase vehicles involving a property crime like auto theft, so I had the rental car company track their vehicle. It was the safer move. I already knew who he was and where he was from. He parked a couple of miles away, ironically back towards the airport. My team and I parked around the corner from the vehicle's location to come up with a strategy since I knew he would try to run. This time I had the Highway Patrol and a couple more vehicles join us. I sent an unmarked police vehicle down to drive by and discovered that the stolen rental vehicle was unoccupied. Long story short, he had gotten picked up by an Uber and taken to the airport, where he flew back to his hometown of Chicago. We had just missed him. I wasn't done with him yet. A few weeks later, the rental car investigator notified me and told me that there was an online reservation made in Phoenix that smelled like our guy. I confirmed with the airline that our suspect was flying to Phoenix that day. I contacted Phoenix airport police and updated them on the suspect, his active warrants, and that he was up to the same crimes heading to Phoenix. They had eyes on him the second he came off the plane. They allowed him to rent the car fraudulently and get into a $100k Cadillac Escalade. He was stopped at the rental exit booth and told to come out of the vehicle, with nowhere he could go in the car. He bailed out on foot and ran straight into a tactical team. Weeks later, I would testify at his probation hearing. The judge was revoking his probation from an earlier case of, yes, you guessed it, rental car fraud. They played my body camera footage from after he took off at the gas station. The judge decided it was time for him to serve out the rest of his eight-year sentence. I felt grateful that the court was finally holding him accountable.

THE WASHED CHECK CAPER

The airport wasn't immune to the same forgery and fraud schemes plaguing the rest of the country—including check washing. For the record, nobody's scrubbing paper with soap. It's a term for stealing a check and altering it to benefit the thief. Mail theft has exploded nationwide, and organized crews are making millions from it. One day, the airport finance department called me. A vendor claimed they hadn't been paid, but finance showed the check as deposited. Digging in, I learned that a post office mailbox near the airport had been broken into recently, and several airport-issued checks had been inside. One of them—for over $13,000—had already been cashed at a local bank. I sent the bank a subpoena for all their records and security video. What I saw made me shake my head. A homeless man in a polo shirt walked into the bank, presented his state-issued ID and the stolen check, and walked out with nearly $14,000 in cash. He wasn't even a customer. I couldn't believe the bank had cashed it. These crews rarely do their own dirty work. They recruit "pawns"—often homeless individuals—to cash the stolen checks for a few hundred bucks. I teamed up with city police and found our check-casher in a tent along the riverbank. He was cooperative and admitted to doing it. He claimed he'd only cashed one or two checks before chickening out, telling the men who recruited him he was sick. The guy claimed he never got paid for the ones he did. He couldn't give me much on the masterminds—just race and sex. I booked him for felony theft but told the DA's office they could knock it down to a misdemeanor. Locking him up for years wouldn't stop the bigger problem, and I knew the airport would never see that $13,000 again. Their best shot at getting any of that money back was to take on the bank that cashed the check.

FRAUD IN THE GOLD BOOTH

It was just after noon when the car rental company called to say they had a fraud suspect standing in their Gold Booth. The man was trying to swap out a rental that had been picked up in Illinois with a stolen corporate account number. By the time my sergeant and I arrived, he was sitting there calm as you please, asking about an exchange. I introduced myself and asked if he knew the vehicle might have been rented fraudulently. He played it off, claiming some other guy had rented the car and he was just driving it. But the details weren't adding up. A security manager told me their corporate accounts had been getting hijacked and used at locations across the country. This guy fit the pattern. When we detained him, he gave his name as K___ G___, but the Illinois driver's license he'd flashed earlier at the counter said K___ S___. Security video even showed him slyly sliding that license down the front of his shorts once the questions started. A quick search of his bag told the rest of the story—Bank of America and Navy Federal debit cards with other people's names on them, two different Social Security cards, and a marijuana grinder for good measure. The banks had already flagged the accounts for fraud. By the end of the day, KG—KS—whoever he wanted to be—was booked for credit card fraud, impersonation, theft of services, drug paraphernalia, and driving on a suspended license. Another case of too many names, not enough sense.

CONTRACTS? WHO NEEDS CONTRACTS?

In 2018, I got a call from a rental car manager who was fed up. She had a stack of video evidence and a sinking suspicion that one of her own employees had turned the rental car garage into a personal chop shop. The employee worked the night shift in the exit booths on the ground floor of the rental car garage at the airport. On video, the manager showed me the play-by-play: First, a young woman stepped out of the employee's personal vehicle, walked across the garage, and climbed into a Hyundai SUV rental. A few seconds later, the exit booth camera caught the employee waving her right through—no contract, no paperwork, nothing. Not long after, the same Hyundai SUV returned. This time, the female suspect was accompanied by a male. They left the Hyundai in the garage, walked over to a white Chevrolet Suburban, and drove it out—again, no contract, no questions asked. A week later, the Suburban came back, and the scam grew. Video showed a different male climbing out of the Suburban and sliding straight into a blue Ford F-150 rental. Once again, the exit booth employee waved both vehicles out like it was business as usual. As if that wasn't enough, management uncovered even more footage: the same employee letting yet another man drive off in an Infiniti sedan without a contract or the company's consent. By then, the manager had seen enough. She wanted her employee prosecuted, and all the vehicles flagged as stolen. Three vehicles were entered into NCIC as stolen. Not long after, OnStar located the missing Suburban in the downtown area. Metro's flex units moved in, made the stop, and arrested the first male and female we saw on video. They didn't deny it—they told officers they had simply paid the rental employee cash to let them drive out of the airport garage with the vehicles. An inside job, caught on camera. And in the rental world, that's about as bad as it gets.

FAKING THE STUB

In 2017, I rode along with a federal agent to speak with the ex-wife of a former airport employee. The interview was part of an ongoing investigation into the ex-employee and suspected theft from airport administration. When government funds are involved, it enters the federal domain, and we typically determine whether state and federal charges should be applied. During our conversation, the ex-wife dropped a new detail: she had learned that her ex-husband had been altering his old airport paycheck stubs to make it look like he was still employed. He wasn't doing it for nostalgia—he was using the phony paperwork to secure cash-advance loans. It turned out the airport had already been getting calls from creditors looking for him. Three stood out: a rental store and two financial loan companies. I followed up, and when I spoke to an employee at one of the loan companies, the picture got clearer. The ex-employee had secured a $5,000 loan from them four months after resigning from the airport by presenting a doctored paycheck stub. The manager handed me a very faded copy of what the man had submitted. He explained that the ex-employee had filled out the application online, then walked into their office near the airport to close the deal. He told them flat-out that he was still employed by the airport, and the loan was approved on the spot. The $5,000 was handed over, and predictably, not a dime had ever been paid back. Multiple attempts to reach him had gone nowhere. In the eyes of the law, he had executed and authenticated a fake document as if it were real, with the clear intent to defraud. That was enough for a felony warrant for criminal simulation. Later, the whole story unraveled. He was eventually arrested on federal charges from a much larger theft investigation, and that's when we learned the real driver behind all of it: a drug habit he and his new girlfriend were feeding to the tune of nearly $300 a day. In the end, he paid the airport back for its loss—which had ballooned into the six figures. Whether the loan companies ever recovered their money is anyone's guess. The girlfriend? She left him after his federal arrest. A few years down the road, I learned she was found deceased from an overdose downtown.

THE $30,000 LESSON

In 2016, a rental car manager called me about a stolen Chevrolet Suburban. At the same time, I learned about a man I'll call K___ W___, who thought he'd just landed the deal of a lifetime. KW told the car rental manager he had paid $30,000 in cash for a Suburban he found on Craigslist. He said the seller, a young man around twenty-two, met him at a McDonald's near the airport. The "deal" was quick: KW handed over the cash, and the seller didn't even bother to count it. He just grabbed the money, jumped into a dark grey Dodge Charger, and took off. KW drove the Suburban home, only to find out the title he'd been given was fake and the vehicle still belonged to the rental company. To top it off, the license plate on it didn't even belong to the Suburban. He asked the rental car company to simply report the Suburban stolen and claim the insurance. Yeah, that wasn't going to happen. The rental manager did some digging of her own and found that the vehicle had been rented the night before at the airport using a counterfeit South Carolina driver's license. She provided photos, and when I pulled the video, I confirmed it was the same guy at the rental counter. Surveillance also showed him and another male arriving on a Southwest flight from Florida. Their trip had actually started in Texas, and they used buddy passes to fly in and out. By the time KW realized he'd been scammed, they were already back in Houston. I filed theft charges against both suspects for the stolen Suburban. Metro Police handled the fraud case for the $30,000, but the victim wasn't eager to explain why he was walking around with that much cash or why he thought a brand-new $75,000 Suburban could really be had for $30,000. It turned out to be a hard—and expensive—lesson in what happens when something looks too good to be true.

CASH, CREDIT, AND A QUICK HAND

In 2018, an email from the airport's parking management company landed in my inbox about a cashier who wasn't just collecting fees—she was running her own side business. They had caught wind of suspicious transactions and sent me copies of receipts that didn't line up with what customers said they'd paid. One customer in July had racked up $184 in parking fees and asked to split the bill between cash and credit. He walked away with a receipt that looked fine. But when the records were checked, his credit card had been charged the full amount. The "missing" cash never made it to the till. When I pulled the video, it showed everything. A short time after the customer left, the cashier pulled bills out of the drawer and set them on top while casually ringing up the next car. She laid a book across the money like she was covering her notes, then—just as smoothly—slid both the book and the cash away in one motion. Sleight of hand, parking lot edition. The audit uncovered other transactions just like it. Big credit card charges where cash had also been paid. By the time we were finished piecing it together, it was clear she'd been skimming steadily, always betting that the paper trail would stop at her receipts. But receipts don't lie, and video doesn't either. She was fired, charged, and walked out the door with no more tricks up her sleeve.

PLASTIC CRIMES AT THE PUMP

Credit card skimmers had been popping up at gas stations all over town—silent little parasites that stole numbers from everyday people at the pump. By early 2018, federal investigators in the area finally had a lead. A couple suspected of placing skimmers were returning a rental car to the airport, and we were asked to keep eyes on them. Federal investigators had already connected the female suspect to fraudulent money orders purchased with stolen card data. She and her partner were bouncing around the city, trying to stay a step ahead of law enforcement. We set up surveillance at the airport. They spent hours inside the terminal, growing frustrated when rental counters turned them away. In that downtime, the female made a critical mistake: she abandoned a blue wallet at the welcome center. Inside were blank magnetic cards—freshly encoded with stolen account numbers. When she came back to report it "lost," she even described the contents herself, calling them "new cards with no names." The arrogance was astonishing We followed them as they left in an Uber to a nearby hotel. The next day, one of the rental car companies worked with us and let the male suspect drive off in a Toyota SUV. Federal agents slipped a tracker onto it, knowing they were dealing with professionals. Sure enough, the surveillance paid off. The male and another associate were caught removing skimmer devices from gas pumps, their operation laid bare in real time. Within a week, we had enough. With a warrant in hand, we assisted federal investigators in hitting their motel room. The search turned up exactly what we expected: skimmers, card encoders, stacks of counterfeit plastic, and other tools of the trade. The room looked like a pop-up factory for financial crime. The female had been cooperative when the door came crashing open, but it didn't matter. She and her partner were hauled off—charged with trafficking in identity theft and criminal simulation. Federal indictments were waiting in the wings. For three days they tried to play the game, walking circles through airports and gas stations. But in the end, their own mistakes—and a forgotten blue wallet—gave them away.

PLASTIC LIES ON THE INTERSTATE

It was a Thursday afternoon in April when metro crime suppression detectives called me about a traffic stop on the interstate not far from the airport. Nothing unusual about that—except the SUV they had pulled over was a shiny new Chevrolet Suburban straight off the Hertz lot at the airport. It had been rented the day before, and already it was overdue. The driver handed over a Florida license with the name *VanDyke*. But inside the car, detectives found something that didn't match the story: a second license, Ohio this time, with VanDyke's face but a different name, Edwards, which was also the name on the car rental agreement. The deeper we dug, the stranger it got. The backpacks we found inside the car were stuffed with debit and credit cards, all embossed with the Edwards name. At first glance they looked like cheap knockoffs—Walmart logos printed on them—but the magnetic strips told the real story. Scanning the cards showed they carried account numbers tied to banks overseas, places like Istanbul and Norway. Credit cards masquerading as debit cards. Counterfeit through and through. VanDyke and his passenger admitted they'd flown in the day before, checked into the Omni downtown, and rented the Suburban with a fake ID. Even the hotel room had been booked with one of the bogus cards. They weren't master criminals by any stretch—just another pair of fraudsters trying to run their scam on borrowed time and stolen plastic. At the end of the day, they were booked, the Suburban went back to Hertz, and another flimsy scheme collapsed under the weight of a cheap hologram and a bad alias.

THE SKY-HIGH SCAM

Over the years, I have worked closely with the corporate security teams of the major airlines. Most of them had prior law enforcement backgrounds, and they were sharp —good at digging into their own employees. If their administrative investigation uncovered criminal activity, they'd hand it over to my division to pursue charges. One case stood out because this girl was living large on the airline's dime. A major airline suspected one of its ticket agents of theft. If you fly often, you've probably seen it: a delay, or an oversold flight, and the ticket agents offer compensation to passengers willing to take a later departure. Done right, it is a legitimate perk. This agent had turned that perk into her personal travel fund. She was issuing compensation tickets worth thousands—to real passengers in the airline's system—but directing those e-tickets to her own email address. Corporate security dug deeper and discovered she'd been using the tickets to fly herself and her boyfriend around and even upgrading her entire family to business and first class on long-haul flights. She'd been at it for over a year, racking up losses of more than $70,000. When they interviewed her, she admitted to some of the theft, but not all. Once they handed the case over, I presented it to the grand jury, which indicted her on one count of theft over $60,000. If convicted, she was looking at six to twelve years in prison. It was a reminder that some scams don't require breaking into a vault—just knowing how to bend the rules from the inside without getting caught. At least until someone notices. Since she was fairly young, I expected a plea deal, but I don't think she was going to get out of a felony conviction. She'll be paying the airline back for most of her adult life.

SELFIES, SCAMS, AND STOLEN RIDES

Our investigative division was working late one afternoon when a call came out about a fraudulent attempt to rent a vehicle at one of the rental counters. We caught up to a male in his 30s who not only had cloned credit cards on his person but also a hand-held encoder he was using on site to reprogram them. That was bold—or maybe just plain dumb. We backtracked his movements before he reached the counter and discovered he'd been dropped off by a young female who parked in the public garage. We located her and the vehicle, and sure enough, she also had contraband tied to identity theft. Both were booked on felony charges, and their cell phones were seized. A search warrant on the phones opened up an entire highlight reel of their crimes. The young woman had a trove of photos of herself posing with high-end rental vehicles—everything from a Jeep to a Mercedes. She clearly thought she was living her best life, but unfortunately for her, the license plates were visible in many of the photos. That was all we needed. The cars were traced back, and sure enough, several were confirmed stolen, three of them from the Memphis airport alone. I contacted investigators in those jurisdictions to compare notes. The couple, originally from the Las Vegas area, already had a history with fraud and auto theft. But standing in our airport, encoding cards on the spot and keeping a whole scrapbook of evidence on their phones? That was some of the boldest—or dumbest —fraud I'd run across.

STRIKE THREE, YOU'RE OUT OF RENTALS

In 2022, Metro Auto Theft detectives reached out about a shipping company that was uneasy about six vehicles set to be shipped overseas to Turkey. The paperwork looked off, and after some digging, it was clear why—the cars belonged to a car rental company and were missing from the rental facility at our airport. The car titles submitted for export were complete forgeries. We went to work pulling LPR hits and video footage from the rental car garage. Between early January and early February, six vehicles had slipped out of the rental car garage. The method was simple, but effective: the suspect piggybacked his way out behind legitimate renters or employees at the exit gates, never drawing attention to himself. The trail led to a name—S___ O___, who was a tow company owner. One of the missing cars had even pinged near his residence. We contacted his family, and eventually he agreed to meet us at the station. To his credit, he cooperated. He told us all six vehicles were sitting at his brother-in-law's auto shop north of town, the very address listed on the shipping company's pickup paperwork. Sure enough, we rolled up with Metro detectives and found five of them parked inside the shop—license plates stripped, batteries disconnected. The sixth turned up at his brother-in-law's home. The brother-in-law insisted he was only "storing" the cars for someone else. He even showed us a picture of the suspect's driver's license he'd saved on his phone. The name on it was no stranger to us—M___J___. MJ had been on our radar before, stealing rentals out of the same rental car garage. This time, one of my counterparts with a neighboring agency tracked him to a youth baseball field, where he was moonlighting as an umpire. When officers moved in to arrest him, he bolted in yet another stolen rental. The car didn't have a tracker, but investigators pinged its onboard Wi-Fi system and quickly located him. MJ was indicted on nearly a dozen felonies—auto theft, fraud, and evading arrest. From piggybacking out of the rental car garage to nearly shipping a half-dozen SUVs overseas, he had built himself a pipeline. But in the end, it was a Wi-Fi signal—and some poor judgment—that brought the entire scheme crashing down.

THE ARMENIAN SKIMMER CREW

In 2016, I was introduced to my first large-scale skimming crew. I got a call from a corporate security investigator from a large financial institution. He told me they were staring down a substantial fraud case: over the course of just a few days, from June 9th through June 12th, several men driving newer model Toyota sedans had hit ATMs across the city for nearly fifty grand in fraudulent withdrawals. The method? Cloned cards—plastic encoded with real customer account numbers that had been stolen.

The investigator suspected the vehicles might be rentals, and he sent me photographs pulled from the bank's cameras. Sure enough, he was right. The silver Toyota seen on video was rented out of my airport in June. A second Camry, also caught on bank video, had been rented out of my airport just a few hours earlier. Both vehicles were conveniently returned on June 12th, right after the spree wrapped up.

The renters turned out to be names that rang plenty of bells in the fraud world. Both had priors involving skimmers and card fraud. They listed California addresses, and I suspected they'd flown in. I reached out to corporate security with the airline and, after a subpoena, confirmed my hunch: they had both come in on a flight from Los Angeles the night before, landing just after midnight—the exact window when the second Camry was picked up.

As I dug deeper, the picture widened. It wasn't just the two of them. There were six men total on the same reservation, all appearing to be of Armenian descent, all from the Glendale/Los Angeles area. Their movement patterns matched crews I'd heard about before—teams that traveled city to city, cloning debit cards, draining accounts, and vanishing before anyone knew what hit them.

The case grew quickly beyond local boundaries. Metro, the Secret Service, and corporate investigators all worked in tandem. Eventually, I learned this crew had worked the entire East Coast, leaving a trail of ATM cash-outs behind them. Federal agents had tracked their movements across state lines, and before long, the entire group was captured and federally indicted.

It was another reminder of how wide the net of fraud can spread—and how something that looks like a local problem can be just one leg of a nationwide operation.

THE LLC HUSTLERS

During the latter end of my career, I was deputized to help with a federal cyber fraud task force and was also heavily involved in a local bank fraud group that comprised bank investigators, federal investigators, and local law enforcement fraud detectives.

Commercial check fraud had been flooding financial

institutions. The scheme was simple but effective—create a shell LLC, walk into a bank with a counterfeit ID, and try to open an account. From there, stolen or counterfeit checks could be deposited, withdrawn, and laundered before anyone knew what hit them.

In July I got a call. A local bank near the airport had flagged a suspicious attempt: a man presenting himself as "Richard Bell" of XYZ LLC. The problem was Richard Bell didn't exist. The ID was fake, and the paperwork was just a cover. When bank staff refused the application, the man walked out, and word quickly spread through the financial investigator network.

Not long after, a second bank reported the same suspect at another branch. This time, he wasn't alone. A second man was waiting in a white Toyota Corolla with California tags. LPR cameras at the airport confirmed what we suspected—the car had been at BNA (Nashville, TN airport) the day before, picking up the same suspect. After backtracking him to the gate and getting some emergency subpoenas, we knew who he was, and that he'd flown in from Texas.

The banks issued bulletins, and by that afternoon, a third bank called: two men, same scam, same paperwork, same fake Illinois driver's license. This time, there were images of both suspects. The second man was immediately recognizable to investigators across the region, a career fraudster with a record of scams that reached into the federal system. I had also arrested him years before in possession of a stolen rental car that was rented fraudulently. He was well known in the banking community.

Both suspects had flown in from Texas. Based on experience, I figured they'd fly back out once they had made their rounds. Sure enough, the Corolla was last seen heading west toward West Tennessee, and the following night both men were booked on a flight back to Dallas. We were waiting.

The arrest at the gate was clean. The search afterward was staggering. Our main fraud guy's carry-on was a portable fraud shop: counterfeit IDs under multiple names, credit cards to match, and paperwork tying him to freshly created LLCs. One counterfeit ID was tied to a check made out for more than $232,000. Even more damning, he had a bank debit card linking that fake identity to a bogus business account.

Suspect 2 carried nearly $8,400 in cash, neatly wrapped in a $10k bank band. A local bank's withdrawal receipt confirmed it had come from one of their fraud accounts just that morning. Another $1,600 was found on our other guy. Altogether, $10,000 was seized and traced back to the scam.

Their sloppiness even tied the web of LLCs back to a nearby apartment address, where our main guy had a newly issued state ID card. It was the same address listed on Syberus LLC—the fake company they'd used to start the whole spree.

By the time it was over, both men were booked for multiple counts of identity theft and forgery. But looking at the stack of IDs, the LLC paperwork, and the sheer volume of checks, it was clear this was just one chapter of a larger story. They weren't small-time check passers—they were LLC hustlers, playing a long game of fraud that spanned states, banks, and identities.

ENGINES, EVASION, AND ARRESTS

The Charger Chase

Some crimes are bold, others reckless—and sometimes they're both.

It was just after lunch when one of the rental car companies called me in a panic. Two Dodge Chargers, one black and one grey, had been driven straight out of their rental area. No paperwork, no keys checked out, nothing. Just two young men behind the wheel, gone before anyone realized what had happened.

By evening, Metro Police were already in hot pursuit of the stolen cars. The grey Charger was the first to surface, tearing through the east side of downtown before the driver bailed out and disappeared into the neighborhood. While officers were still hunting him, the black Charger drove right into their perimeter, trying to pick up the buddies who had bailed from the grey car.

That one didn't get far. After a wild chase, it screeched to a halt, and the three suspects scattered like rabbits. Officers scooped them up one by one—two caught ducking into a nearby restaurant, the third hiding behind a house.

Back at the precinct, the stories unraveled fast. One suspect admitted he'd been driving but quickly tried to shift the blame. Another clammed up. The third denied everything. Metro confirmed at least two of them were Crip gang members, which explained the fear and finger-pointing in the interview room.

In the end, all three were charged—felony theft, felony evading, and misdemeanor evading. Both Chargers were recovered, battered but intact. The original driver of the grey car slipped away, but for the rest, the chase was over.

What struck me about this case wasn't just the chase itself, but the sheer arrogance. Broad daylight, gang members taking two brand-new Chargers from a busy rental lot, like nobody would notice. And then driving right into a police perimeter to try to rescue their friends —it was reckless, but also telling. Sometimes it wasn't just the crime that caught my attention, it was the mindset behind it.

THE HELLCAT HUSTLE

A few summers before I retired, we got hit hard with auto thefts in the parking garages and surface lots. The thieves had very specific taste: high-end Dodge Hellcats, Scat Packs, and Shelby Chargers. All of them had supercharged engines—and all of them were hot commodities for organized theft crews.

One suspect made our job easier by being dumb enough to stop and pay the parking fee. That gave us a perfect shot of his face. He was later identified as a longtime auto theft suspect out of Memphis. When I called their auto theft unit, they told me he had outstanding warrants and even a good phone number. But there was a catch—their judges wouldn't sign a warrant to ping his phone because it was "only a property crime." That was frustrating. If officers have probable cause and a ping will catch a suspect, the warrant should be signed. Period.

Since I wasn't bound by Memphis' rules, I got my own tracking warrant signed. I started feeding GPS updates to the metro auto theft team and other investigators who had pegged him in their cases. One day, city auto theft spotted a Dodge Ram TRX—another supercharged favorite— right where the phone had him. Sure enough, the truck was stolen. They kept it under surveillance, arrested the driver, and found a stolen gun from one of our airport thefts inside.

Two days later, the pings put my guy back in the same area. Detectives saw him in another stolen Dodge, but he spotted surveillance and took off toward Memphis. He didn't make it far—another agency spiked his tires and used a PIT maneuver, sending him crashing out.

In custody, he spilled. He was part of a major crew stealing Dodge vehicles across at least three states, with losses in the millions. He was federally indicted along with dozens of others. Our airport cases ended up being some of the strongest evidence in the federal file.

The Dodge vehicles were easy targets. You could go on Amazon, buy a programmer with blank key fobs, break a window, and within minutes have a car running. Another suspect in this same crew was caught up north after a pursuit. Detectives found his programmer in the trunk with VIN numbers from most of the stolen vehicles already stored inside. It was a brilliant piece of evidence to have.

Our work at the airport wasn't just about one stolen car in a garage—it was part of taking down a multimillion-dollar crew. To know the evidence we gathered played a role in that indictment was one of the best finishes to an investigation in my career.

THE ROGUE RIDE AND BUMPER LOCK

Some people just can't take a hint—or, in this case, a direct order from the police department. A local taxi driver had recently had his taxi license pulled, meaning he was officially barred from taking fares for his company. But that didn't stop him. He kept showing up at the airport, picking up passengers like nothing had changed.

Patrol officers warned him, and I even entered his plate into the LPR system. The second time he showed up after the warning, he spotted a police car nearby and bolted. He didn't realize we were tracking his plate—but if he saw a patrol unit, he wouldn't stop either. That's when I decided it was time for our team to step in.

The next time he rolled in, he was mid-drop-off with several passengers in the cab when he noticed a patrol car behind him. The officer in that car didn't even know who he was; he just happened to be driving by. But the driver panicked, hit the gas, and took off—with his passengers still inside.

The riders gave him an earful, and he eventually dumped them, bags and all, in the parking lot of a nearby restaurant. By then, we were tailing him in unmarked vehicles. When he stopped in a turn lane, we moved in. One of my investigators pulled bumper-to-bumper in front of him; another did the same behind. Bumper lock. It's a precision maneuver—when you're touching both ends of the vehicle, it can't go forward or backward, and you minimize damage to everyone's cars. My guys were trained for it, and they executed it perfectly.

The cabbie lost it. He jumped out screaming, refused commands, and fought for several minutes before a five-second burst from a Taser changed his mind. Having volunteered to take a Taser hit during training, I can tell you—those are the longest five seconds of your life.

He was arrested for evading police, resisting arrest, and trespassing. The local licensing commission confiscated his taxi and banned him from ever doing business at the airport again. As for the passengers he abandoned, they just wanted to catch their flight.

All of this was so unnecessary. A man willing to risk his passengers, fight the police, and lose everything—all for a fare. It was a reminder that sometimes the most reckless acts aren't about money or gangs or drugs. Sometimes, it's just stubbornness that pushes someone over the line.

MUSTANG TO MEXICO

Rental car thefts at the airport had always felt like a cat-and-mouse game, but in early 2024 the cats got bold. In January, a man strolled up to the National counter with a Mexican driver's license under the name "Abel Rangel." The ID looked legitimate enough, but the man in front of the counter was actually C__ R__—someone we already knew from earlier thefts. This time he drove away in a brand-new 2024 convertible Ford Mustang with temporary tags.

A couple weeks later, I pulled the video. CR hadn't traveled alone. He flew in from Texas with two other men, both carrying Mexican IDs, all part of the same crew. They started their trip in Harlingen, connected through Dallas, and landed at BNA just long enough to pick up the Mustang before heading south again.

By February 7, the car's trail ended over 1,500 miles away in Colima, Mexico. That Mustang had crossed the border almost as quickly as it had rolled off the rental lot. We entered it into NCIC, but everyone knew it wasn't coming back soon.

The deeper we dug, the more it became clear this wasn't a one-off theft. Homeland Security, CBP, and investigators from airports across the country were already on their trail. These crews were moving from city to city, presenting counterfeit Mexican IDs, and bleeding rental agencies dry. When Texas authorities finally caught one of them, the suspect cooperated. He gave up names, travel patterns, and how they funneled cars south into Mexico.

For us, it confirmed what we suspected: this was a highly organized ring operating across U.S. airports. This Mustang was a reminder that even a single theft at our airport could be part of something much larger. Cases like that always stuck with me, because they showed how local work could ripple out and matter far beyond our city.

THE WALK-ON CAR THIEF

It was just before sunrise in the month of May when Enterprise's risk supervisor called me in a panic. One of their vehicles had vanished from the rental car garage without so much as a contract, a booth swipe, or a trace on our LPR cameras. The license plate she gave me wasn't showing up anywhere, so I pulled footage from inside the garage. Sure enough, I spotted the missing car slipping out from the second floor like a ghost.

The still photo I grabbed was all the confirmation Enterprise needed—it was their car. What puzzled me was how it had been taken. No paperwork, no gate exit. Just gone.

By the afternoon, the mystery unraveled. Neighboring law enforcement authorities called to say the car had already been impounded. The driver had been arrested, and his mugshot told the rest of the story. He was the same man I'd caught earlier on our own airport cameras, loitering near the Enterprise counter before helping himself to a car. When I backtracked the video, it became even clearer. He hadn't come in on a flight or with friends. He had walked in on foot, straight off the main roadway that ran in front of the airport, and wandered into the rental car garage. From there, it was just a matter of timing. As soon as the Enterprise booth was left unattended, this guy seized the chance. One unguarded vehicle, one unlocked opportunity—and he drove right out.

He didn't make it far. By the time Enterprise realized what had happened, he was sitting in a county jail cell.

It was a reminder that not all thieves need elaborate scams or counterfeit IDs. Sometimes, they just walk in off the street and take what's sitting in front of them if the opportunity presents itself.

FROM THE STATE PARK TO THE STATE LINE

Some thefts start small—a broken car window, a stolen wallet—but quickly spiral into something bigger.

In August, a woman's purse was stolen while she was walking at a nearby state park. Inside were her driver's license and credit cards. A month later, those same items turned up at the airport—used by a suspect to rent a shiny 2015 Buick Enclave from Dollar/Thrifty.

By October, the FBI was on my line. The Buick had surfaced hundreds of miles away in Taylor, Michigan. When local police tried to pull it over, the suspect hit the gas. The chase didn't last long. The vehicle was boxed in, and he and his passenger were arrested.

Taylor detectives wanted the SUV officially listed as stolen so they could tack on auto theft charges. Dollar/Thrifty's manager brought me the paperwork, and even though the vehicle had already been recovered, the case was buttoned up.

What started as a wallet theft on a quiet Tennessee trail had turned into a multi-state pursuit, stolen identity, stolen vehicle, and two men in custody. It goes to show how fast things can escalate—how one missing wallet can set much bigger wheels in motion.

THE TEST DRIVE THAT NEVER CAME BACK

Car sales and rentals have one thing in common: trust. And sometimes that trust is misplaced.

Hertz Corporate Security called me about a Dodge Challenger that had vanished during what was supposed to be a routine test drive. A man walked onto their sales lot next to the airport one evening with a young woman he claimed was his daughter. He said he wanted to buy her a car, and the Challenger caught his eye.

The "daughter" handed over a Missouri driver's license, and the sales agent, thinking it all checked out, handed them the keys. What he didn't do was confirm the man's identity. The Challenger rolled off the lot that night and never returned.

Within days, license plate readers picked it up outside St. Louis, Missouri. By the time we connected the dots, Hazelwood police had already stopped the car, arrested the occupants on other charges, and had it towed to a local impound.

The names on the Missouri licenses matched the suspects: the young woman who posed as the buyer and her accomplice, the man who'd pretended to be her father. Their photos lined up perfectly with Hertz's surveillance footage.

Hertz could get their car back, but only after a trip to Missouri and plenty of paperwork. As for the suspects, they turned what was supposed to be a test drive into a theft—and a reminder of how quickly misplaced trust can turn into opportunity for someone willing to exploit it.

CAMPUS GETAWAY

In 2018, a rental car security investigator called me about two vehicles that had gone missing from their fleet. A male had come through the airport, presented a driver's license under the name "R___ B___," and drove off with not one, but two cars. For a while, it looked like a routine overdue rental. Then the bank flagged the credit card he'd used—it didn't belong to him. The charges were blocked, and the rental company realized they'd been scammed. Both cars were reported stolen.

One of the vehicles was equipped with a tracking device, which showed it sitting at a nearby university campus in another jurisdiction. Local investigators were called in, and when they found the car, it wasn't just a stolen rental sitting in the lot. A search turned up drugs inside the vehicle, which led school officials to take a closer look at the suspect's dorm room. Sure enough, more drugs were found there too.

The suspect wasn't around when the car was located and towed, and I made sure the rental company knew their second vehicle was still outstanding. That one eventually turned up back at the airport about a week later, likely returned quietly once the heat was on.

This kid's bad decision snowballed. A fake ID and a stolen car turned into a campus drug investigation that probably cost him his education. He thought he was running rentals; in reality, he was running out of time.

DYSFUNCTIONAL DUO

In early 2017, I was sitting in my office when the phone rang. On the other end was a manager from a local car sales business, his voice sharp with urgency. A white female had just pulled onto his lot in a red Kia SUV, hopped out, and jumped straight into one of his cars—a black 2011 Dodge Charger. She didn't work there, he didn't know her, and he sure hadn't given her permission to take off with the car. Last he saw, she was headed for Interstate 40.

The manager told me the Charger had a GPS tracker

on it, and right then it was pinging at the cab holding area of the airport. I got his information, notified patrol units, and a few minutes later dispatch confirmed they had eyes on a Charger in the exact spot.

When I pulled up, the Charger was still there, idling, with a white female behind the wheel. As soon as I lit her up, she started climbing out. I got out of my unit, weapon drawn, and gave her commands. She complied, stepping backward toward me, where I cuffed her without incident.

She was identified as Chassidy, carrying nothing but an expired Alabama license. I read her her Miranda rights, and she talked.

Her story tumbled out in pieces. The Kia SUV she'd left at the dealership? Rented by her mother in Tampa. According to Chassidy, her mom had picked her up in West Virginia a couple days earlier. The two of them were driving to Alabama when an argument blew up somewhere on I-40 in Tennessee. Chassidy said she told her mom to get out, left her standing on the shoulder of the interstate, and kept driving. She slept in the Kia overnight, then pulled into the auto sales lot the next morning and decided she liked the Dodge Charger better.

As for the rear-end damage on the Kia? She shrugged and admitted it happened in Knoxville, TN, but said she drove away from the scene before anyone could stop her. I called a Highway Patrol contact in Knoxville to check for hit-and-runs that matched her timeline.

In the end, Chassidy was arrested for auto theft and driving without a license. The dealership employee came and picked up the Charger from the airport, while the Kia —still banged up from Knoxville—was collected by the rental company.

It was one of those cases where the truth was stranger than the fiction: a fight with mom on the side of the highway, a stolen car swap in the city, and a last stop in our car lot.

GRAND THEFT: EXOTIC EDITION

Metro PD transferred a call to our investigation unit involving a stolen Audi R8—definitely not your typical car theft. I got in touch with the owner of a company that leased exotic vehicles. He explained the car had been dropped off at the airport for a renter to pick up, but shortly after, they discovered the driver's license and insurance information used to secure the rental were completely fraudulent.

This kind of scam was common with traditional rental car companies, but now it was spreading to exotic rental operations. We reviewed surveillance footage and confirmed the person who picked up the Audi wasn't the person who was supposed to be renting it. Unfortunately, we couldn't identify him, and the vehicle's GPS tracker had been disabled. I believe the car was eventually recovered in another state with a swapped VIN plate—classic move.

Not long after, I assisted the same company again—this time involving a Lamborghini. The lead came from an unlikely source: a young woman who had seen the car before it disappeared. The man driving it—an older guy—had approached her at a gas station and tried to hit on her, despite being old enough to be her grandfather. She declined, but he left a phone number.

That number turned out to be a goldmine. I ran it

through a pawn shop database and matched it to someone out of state who was a regular customer at local pawn shops. I confirmed his identity and passed the information to the metro PD, who had jurisdiction on the case.

Before this, I didn't even know these exotic rental car companies existed. They're scattered across the U.S., and the business model is risky. Most of them don't own the vehicles, they manage rentals on behalf of the owners. And because insurance companies typically don't allow subleasing, there's always a question of coverage if one of these high-end cars is stolen. It's a glamorous business on the surface, but underneath, it's full of liabilities and fraud opportunities.

CAMARO, CREDIT CARDS, AND THE DAIRY QUEEN STAKEOUT

In 2017, I was knee-deep in a follow-up investigation tied to two suspects our night shift had arrested earlier that morning. They'd been running the usual scam—fraudulent driver's licenses paired with stolen credit card numbers—to slip rental cars out of the car rental lot.

I called the car rental manager and told him I had reason to believe they'd walked out with a Chevrolet Camaro two days earlier. The manager checked the records and confirmed it: the Camaro had been rented with a bogus Illinois license under the name we suspected. The license number was fake, and the address matched the other counterfeit licenses we'd already seized. That car was as good as stolen, and I had it entered into NCIC.

I got OnStar involved. They pinged the stolen car and patched in local PD to intercept it. I gave them my cell number so they could loop me in once they had eyes on the Camaro.

Not long after, an officer called. He'd found the Camaro sitting unattended behind a Dairy Queen. As he approached, three or four males sitting next door at Long John Silver's spotted him. The second they made eye contact, they bolted—jumping into a silver Nissan SUV and tearing out of the lot.

Minutes later, witnesses phoned in to report a suitcase tossed from that same SUV. Officers recovered it: a carry-on packed with a credit card embossing machine. A couple minutes after that, another call came in—someone had seen a man sprinting down a side street. Officers detained him and brought him back.

The runner turned out to be one of our male suspects carrying an Illinois license. Witnesses ID'd him as the one they'd just seen on foot. Backtracking his path, officers recovered more than twenty magnetic stripe cards—some blank, others embossed. One of them carried the exact number used to rent the Camaro at the airport.

Back at the station, the suspect on foot stuck to the script. He claimed he knew nothing about the cards scattered along his escape path or the embosser dumped from the SUV. But we both knew the odds of coincidence didn't stretch that far.

I'd worked plenty of fraud cases that ended in a courtroom or a jail cell, but this one unraveled in the parking lot of a Dairy Queen. For all their fake IDs and embossing machines, their downfall looked more like a bad sitcom than organized crime.

THE RENTAL DUKES OF HAZZARD

Some mornings you walk into the office and know it's going to be an interesting day. This was one of those mornings. Patrol had called in a heavily damaged rental car. The frame was bent, the body was crumpled, and it was parked in one of the rental company's lots, completely unoccupied.

After a little digging, I learned the company had been storing overflow vehicles in an adjacent lot that sat about six to eight feet higher than the one where we found the wreck. The two lots were separated by a six-foot chain-link fence.

Reviewing the footage told the story. The driver had been traveling way too fast in the upper lot, lost control, and literally ran out of asphalt. The car cleared the fence—all six feet of it—before slamming into the lower lot and coming to rest, totaled.

Whoever was behind the wheel didn't stick around to explain. He walked away before anyone could get his name. But with some investigation, we eventually identified him.

I've seen plenty of wrecked rental cars, but this one went airborne like a scene straight out of *The Dukes of Hazzard*. I only wish we'd caught the actual jump on video. Something tells me the rental agreement didn't cover "flight."

FROM RINGS TO RUNWAYS

FELONY LANE INTERCEPT

OVER A DECADE, I OFTEN GOT ROPED INTO investigations surrounding a group called the Felony Lane Gang. You can google the name and find dozens of stories across the United States. The group originates in southern Florida, and they travel all over the country breaking into vehicles at gyms, parks, churches, and anywhere they think a woman will leave her purse behind. Once they get the purse, they will recruit females to dress up as the burglary victim and go to banks and use the victim's ID and checks to make withdrawals. The suspects who facilitated this were always male, and they would often travel in different vehicles than the female suspects they recruited. Sometimes they would bring females with them from Florida; other times they would recruit the females in whatever city they just happened to land. These females were typically homeless or had substance abuse problems. This group often operated out of rental cars, and that's how I got pulled into the investigations. In one case involving FLG (Flagstaff, AZ airport), I was able to identify a rental SUV with Texas plates as a suspect vehicle involved in some area auto burglaries. I was sitting at my desk in my office and happened to look at the cameras in the rental car garage and spotted the same black Toyota SUV with the Texas plate. Another detective and I went over to the garage, and I turned on my blue lights since it was illegally parked in a lane of traffic. I immediately smelled marijuana in the vehicle and had the driver exit. Once more officers arrived on the scene, the driver attempted to flee on foot, but we took him to the ground and handcuffed him. Inside the SUV were checkbooks, IDs, and wallets of multiple female victims, along with wigs to provide the female suspects for the banks. I reviewed more video footage after the arrest and figured out he was at the airport dropping off another male suspect, who left the airport in a different rental car. I assume the second rental car was for the girls to go to the banks in. By the time we caught onto it, he had gone to the hotel and picked up two female suspects and left the area. To this day, they continue to operate in states all over the US doing the same thing. They are getting caught more with the help of technology like LPR cameras, but as long as they can make a little money, they'll keep doing it. This was a great hit because we caught them before they started doing bank transactions in the area. Even better, they still had the stolen property in the vehicle. Several agencies, including the FBI, stepped in to help after we made the initial arrest. These cases can be frustrating because the males usually only get hit with the auto burglaries. The females get charged with the heavier crimes like identity theft, forgery, and theft. I helped several agencies with this crew, and often the female suspects were promised drugs in return for their bank services. Right before I retired, I encouraged several agencies to use their states' human trafficking laws against the males. That would carry heavier penalties and maybe keep them locked up longer. If you learn anything from this story, it's never to leave your valuables behind in the car, especially somewhere they expect you to do so, like a gym or park.

COAST-TO-COAST PICKPOCKETS

One of the best theft cases I ever worked involved a crew of national pickpockets who came into town during a large city event. These weren't amateurs—they were professionals who ran their own counter-surveillance, always on the lookout for cops who might be tailing them. Their operation was slick. One or two women carried oversized purses to stash the wallets and phones lifted from unsuspecting victims in crowded areas. They'd fly in on a Friday and leave by Sunday, often shipping the stolen property out separately to avoid being caught with it. But they made a mistake during their departure from our airport. One of them used a stolen debit card at a retail shop inside the terminal. That transaction gave me everything I needed. I tracked the crew to their flight—they were all booked under the same reservation—and identified every one of them. I sent subpoenas to major airlines, asking for alerts if any of them traveled again. Just a couple weeks later, one airline notified me that the same crew was booked to fly to a major city in Texas. I contacted that city, and their downtown police district responded by plastering the suspects' photos all over the area. A few weeks later, the crew flew again—this time to Coachella in California. Several members were arrested leaving the venue with stolen wallets and phones. For months, I tracked their movements, notifying every city they visited. One agency in the Northeast even stopped them at the airport and told them to turn around and fly back to Florida, where they were based. It was rewarding to hear stories from the agencies I contacted—many of whom made arrests or intercepted the crew based on those tips. Let this serve as a warning: when you're in a packed entertainment district, drink responsibly and guard your valuables. All it takes is a bump in a crowd, and your phone or wallet is gone—sold overseas by the time you even realize it.

CLOSING THE LANE

In 2019, a detective from a neighboring jurisdiction called me about a rental car tied to an auto burglary that had just gone down in one of their city parks. The victim's vehicle had been broken into, and witnesses pointed them to a late-model white Chevrolet Equinox. It came back to a rental company, so I got in touch with one of their corporate investigators. Given the urgency, they tracked the SUV for us and provided its location.

I first spotted it south of town and pulled in Metro for backup. A Metro detective eventually found the Equinox and lit it up in a Walgreens parking lot. The driver bolted the second the car stopped but didn't make it far—detectives from both agencies ran her down.

Inside the vehicle, we found the usual Felony Lane starter kit: multiple driver's licenses from Tennessee and Georgia, all stolen during auto burglaries, along with a stack of gift cards. Those were almost certainly bought using stolen credit and debit cards along with the IDs.

For anyone unfamiliar, the Felony Lane Gang is a loosely organized crime group that travels from state to state breaking into cars—usually at parks, gyms, and daycare centers—snatching purses and wallets. They're notorious for quickly using stolen IDs and bank cards to drain accounts, often through drive-thru bank lanes. Their name comes from their habit of using the "felony lane"— the farthest outside lane at the bank (at banks that used to have or still have multiple drive through service lanes)—so the teller has a harder time seeing who's behind the wheel.

The woman behind the wheel of our rental turned out to be the renter of the Equinox. She was booked by the neighboring jurisdiction, and the case was folded into their investigation. Another Felony Lane crew had rolled into town thinking they could make quick money running smash-and-grabs. Instead, they ended up caught flat-footed in a Walgreens lot—stopped cold by quick coordination and shared resources. Most of the time, Felony Lane cases were like chasing ghosts—stolen checks, stolen rentals, and suspects already long gone. But this time, the trap worked exactly the way we planned. Watching them fall into it was one of the more satisfying moments of my career.

THE RABBIT BEDDING TRAFFICKERS

One of the strangest drug cases I ever handled didn't involve real drugs—at least, not much. Two guys from the Northeast had flown into town for a big event. While they were here, they made a little side money with a scam. We didn't know that part yet—all we knew was that a patrol officer on the terminal ramp had found one of their checked bags broken open. Inside were a dozen vacuum-sealed packages. They looked exactly like the wrapping you see in major drug seizures. Our narcotics K9 alerted on them immediately. We tracked the owners down in the concourse and escorted them to an office below. They consented to a search, and sure enough, we found a pound of marijuana in one of the bags. The rest of the vacuum-sealed packages? Filled with shredded cardboard bedding—the kind you use in rabbit or hamster cages. After a long interview, they explained the plan: show a buyer the real marijuana, claim they had "tons more," and then sell the rest as these sealed bags of rabbit bedding. They'd lined up a deal with a couple of shady locals who were ready to hand over thousands of dollars. The deal fell apart when the buyers wanted to open the packages before paying. Spooked, our two scammers grabbed their stuff and bolted to the airport. They offered to help us set up the would-be buyers, so we ran with it. The buyers drove for over an hour to meet at a location we controlled. When they showed up with the cash, we detained them and seized the money as drug proceeds. The two fake-drug sellers got a citation and were sent on their way back home. It was the only time in my career I ever busted someone for selling marijuana—and hamster bedding.

FELONY LANE TRAINING DAY

In the spring of 2021, I got a call from a longtime friend and investigator from a neighboring agency. He had a Nissan SUV tied to a string of auto burglaries earlier that day, and the method had Felony Lane Gang written all over it.

I jumped on the LPR cameras and, sure enough, the same Nissan had been spotted in another jurisdiction between 9:00 and 10:40 that morning. A quick phone call confirmed it—they'd had auto burglaries, too. While scanning through the LPR hits, I noticed a white Chevy Malibu tailing the Nissan in both places, like a shadow car. Both were rentals from the same company.

The Malibu turned out to be fraudulently rented with a woman's stolen ID. She'd had her purse stolen at a ballpark in Arkansas, and now her driver's license was playing chauffeur to a criminal crew. With that information in hand, we were able to get the car listed as stolen due to fraud.

Not long after, both the Nissan and the Malibu ran from police in yet another jurisdiction. The Malibu was entered into NCIC and OnStar was looped in. Later that afternoon, the car turned up in Kentucky. OnStar shut it down when officers moved in.

Inside were four suspects—the female driver, who had the stolen ID sitting in her purse, and three teenage boys who were clearly being groomed as the next generation of Felony Lane Gang players. They thought they were in some kind of masterclass, but their "training day" ended with a ride to jail. It wasn't just stolen IDs and cars—it was watching a criminal network recruit the next generation.

Catching them mattered, but seeing kids being taught to follow in those footsteps made me realize how deep the problem really went.

THE UGLY SHOES CASE

One morning when I arrived at the office, my team was in a frenzy. Patrol officers had responded to the small regional airport we had jurisdiction over and took reports of several aircraft that had been burglarized. The GPS units and transponders that were stolen from them are hot on the international market. Once they're out of US jurisdiction, it is hard to recover them, and they go for top dollar anywhere from $8k to $20k depending on the make, model, etc. I started reviewing video of the area, and I determined the suspect arrived in a red Volvo sedan. He had removed his license plate to avoid detection from our LPR cameras, but I had the make, model, and color. What was interesting about the suspect was his outfit. Although he covered his head and face, he was wearing a dark pullover hoodie, khaki shorts, and these ugly black shoes with a large red "V" on the side. We got as much information as we could, and I blasted a BOLO out to airports all over the US, because the vehicle he was using stood out. I received a call the next day from an FBI agent out of Baltimore. He did not think our suspect was on his radar, but he advised me that two other small private airports in Ohio had also been hit a day or two before our airport, and the vehicle was the same, a red Volvo sedan. I reached out to the law enforcement agencies that investigated those cases, and they sent me some good video, and sure enough, it was our guy in the hoodie, same khaki shorts, and same ugly shoes. I searched LPR cameras within a 25-mile radius of our small airport and filtered the search to red Volvo sedans. One came up that stood out; it had Ohio plates. I knew our guy wasn't local, so I dove into this Ohio license plate. Sure enough, LPR cameras near the two other private airports in Ohio had picked up the same red Volvo with the same license plate around the time of their burglaries. The two small airports in Ohio were hit hard, with 23 aircraft burglarized within 24 hours. We were lucky; only 5 aircraft were affected. I started tracking this red Volvo on LPRs - Illinois, Missouri, Colorado; he was traveling west. Over the following weekend, it hit several LPR cameras along a highway stretch in Missouri coming back towards Tennessee, and I saw an opportunity. I contacted the Missouri Highway Patrol, and a trooper caught up to the car and made a traffic stop. He called my cell phone at the scene and told me that the driver gave consent to search the car, but no aviation equipment was located. Then it struck me. I sent a text to the trooper's cell phone with photos of the suspect's wardrobe on the night of the burglaries. Minutes later, the trooper sends me a pic of khaki shorts, a dark hoodie, and those ugly shoes sitting in the trunk of the suspect's car. The suspect saw the trooper take pictures of his clothes, then immediately revoked his consent to search the car any further. It was too late. I got felony theft and burglary warrants issued that day, and the district attorney's office approved extradition back to Tennessee. As far as I know, he's still sitting in jail today. Once his case is settled in court locally, he will be transported to Ohio, where he can answer the rest of the charges. This was a great needle-in-a-haystack case. Our video footage from the smaller airport was not that great, but it was enough to tell the vehicle was a red sedan. The LPR cameras only caught the taillights, but the taillights of a Volvo are unique, so we could confirm the make, model, and color. Although our two airports had LPR cameras, the metro city where our airports lie did not. A small town just north of the city limits did. This small town was where he had come through earlier that day before the burglaries happened. It was that one LPR camera in the small city just north that buried this guy. I know people have their concerns about privacy and LPR, but I can't stress enough how much they help law enforcement with crimes across the spectrum.

PLEA DEAL DISGRACE

The closest I ever came to shooting a suspect in my career started with a longtime felon in a stolen rental car. We tracked him to a garage on the west side of town, attached to an apartment complex. I was in my unmarked sedan with another sergeant, both of us wearing tactical gear. As the suspect backed into a parking space, I pulled up just to his right—enough room for him to exit—lit up my blue lights and opened my door. That's when he gunned it forward, wheels cranked toward me, and slammed into my driver's door. Thank God I hadn't stepped out yet. He backed up, smashed into the car beside him, then shot out of the garage. My weapon was already up—if he'd hit my door again, it would have been a deadly force situation. The adrenaline was through the roof.

He fled from city officers too, and they eventually broke off the pursuit. But we knew who he was and where he lived. The next day, city PD moved in to serve the warrants I'd taken out: aggravated assault on an officer, auto theft, felony evading, and more.

From inside the apartment, officers could hear movement—the sound of things being tossed. When they entered, he tried to bull his way through a wall of cops. That didn't work. Meanwhile, others in the apartment were tossing bags of drugs and guns off the balcony. The case was solid. But when trial day came, the DA's office cut a deal during jury selection—no felony convictions. I couldn't believe it. I was ready to put him away, but in a big city, sometimes it's about clearing the docket, not justice.

Seven years later, I got a call from a friend in a neighboring agency. They were about to serve a search warrant and asked if I wanted to go. The target? Same guy. Still into drugs, stolen cars, and violent crime. The SWAT team made entry. He resisted and got put face-down on the floor. Inside were a second man, a woman, and a small child. The house was barebones—mattresses on the floor, a few guns, drugs—but the garage was loaded: a stolen Corvette, a stolen Dodge Ram TRX, and over ninety pounds of marijuana.

About a year later, I heard he was wanted on multiple federal charges. The feds finally caught up with him and found him with a self-inflicted gunshot wound. He was finally off the streets, but that plea deal from years earlier still stings. The justice system isn't perfect—I get plea bargains have their place—but that one never should have happened.

GRINDR GOTCHA

It was the middle of summer when I first came across him—a man running rental car fraud out of the airport while also stealing from hotels. Metro police were already looking at him for swiping a briefcase from a lobby. I got involved when our airport LPR cameras hit on the car he'd fraudulently rented.

We caught him dropping another man at the terminal, trying to set him up with a counterfeit driver's license for a fresh rental. When patrol officers moved in, he stomped the gas and fled at high speed. The car was entered into NCIC as stolen.

A couple of days later, Georgia state police tried to stop him. He crashed during the pursuit, bailed out, and vanished into the woods. Left behind in the wreck was another stunned passenger, along with laptops, counterfeit IDs, and stacks of fraud evidence. That crash finally gave us enough to put a name to the suspect. Turned out, he was already wanted by the U.S. Marshals in Missouri—he'd cut off an ankle monitor while awaiting trial on federal fraud charges.

We weren't the only ones closing in. Metro had a working phone number for him, left over from their briefcase case. I drafted a warrant to ping the phone, and it kept lighting up near the Doubletree Hotel downtown. We set up surveillance, and sure enough, there he was—sitting on the curb, glued to his cell phone swiping through a dating app, completely unaware. We took him into custody right there. We received good pings sporadically over a couple of days at the hotel, and we realized he would leave his room each day to sit outside the hotel and smoke a cigarette. My team and I rolled up during one of those times.

In his pocket was a hotel room key, so we wrote another warrant. On the way up, we ran into a jittery man in the hallway. He admitted our suspect had lured him there through a dating app and asked him to bring drugs. We found the stash on him, cut him loose, and moved on.

Inside the room was the real prize: a laptop, tablet, printer, piles of counterfeit documents, and evidence of more identity theft. There was even another set of rental car keys, proof he'd already lined up his next fraudulent ride.

This guy never stopped moving—not after a wrecked car, not after federal charges, not even with the Marshals hunting him. But when his phone betrayed his hiding spot, the run was over. Booked on local fraud, with a federal hold to drag him back to Missouri, he finally ran out of road.

Another memorable case and one of the last ones I worked together with Detective BW. I recall speaking with the US Attorney's Office out of St. Louis and they were astonished that airport PD detectives were so aggressive at catching this guy. I jokingly told them I was happy to save their US Marshals some work. It was pretty astonishing that this guy had the gall to cut off a federal ankle monitor, flee the state, and dive neck deep right back into fraud, auto theft, and getting into pursuits with law enforcement. There were some drugs involved, but that was not the motivator. He was smart, with a technical background, but he used his skill set on the wrong side of the law, which blew my mind. I have no doubt he could have landed a good job.

FLIGHT RISK TURNED FELON TRAIL

We were investigating an individual who came through the security checkpoint with a large amount of cash. His story didn't add up. A quick check revealed he'd recently been arrested in the Midwest while driving with a substantial quantity of narcotics in his vehicle.

We seized the money as suspected drug proceeds, along with his cell phone. Once we obtained a search warrant for the phone, the full scope of his operation came into view.

Text messages revealed he was mentoring a local convicted felon—recently released on parole—on how to set up a company bank account specifically for laundering drug money. The phone also contained photos of large quantities of narcotics and contraband we believed had recently been transferred to the parolee.

We coordinated with the state's probation and parole office, and their investigators arranged a visit to the parolee's apartment. The moment we arrived, the strong smell of raw marijuana hit us at the door. A woman answered and claimed the parolee no longer lived there.

Over the next two hours, investigators spoke with him by phone several times. Eventually, he stuck to the story that he didn't live there anymore. We weren't buying it—and neither was the judge who issued the search warrant.

Inside the apartment, we found a significant stash of drugs, a couple of assault-style rifles, a handgun, and additional evidence tying him to ongoing drug activity.

Cases like this often begin with something minor at the airport, but they can quickly unfold into much larger, multi-agency investigations. I can't stress enough how many of our investigations started small, but opened up a can of worms like you wouldn't believe. One suspicious passenger at a checkpoint led to guns, drugs, and a felon headed back to prison. It was a reminder that airports aren't just points of travel—they're crossroads for criminal networks, and sometimes, that's exactly where they get tripped up.

INSIDE JOBS

CLOCKING IN, DRIVING OUT

Rental car thefts are usually crimes of opportunity, but every so often you run into someone who knows the system well enough to exploit it from the inside.

Rental car management called me about a former employee who was back at it again. He'd already been fired for stealing one of their vehicles, but now he was seen driving another—a white Volvo sedan that hadn't been returned. Video told the rest of the story. On the night before he was officially let go, he used his employee codes to slip the Volvo out of the rental lot undetected. From there, he drove it to another garage on airport property, got out, and let someone else drive it away. A week later, cameras caught him climbing in and out of the same Volvo, using it as a shuttle to and from the airport like it was his personal car.

And it didn't stop with the Volvo. Two more SUVs—a

pair of BMWs—were taken the same way. Sometimes he drove, sometimes he rode shotgun, but the pattern was always the same: get the vehicle past the exit gate, park it in another garage, and hand it off. Then, as if nothing had happened, he'd walk back into the rental counter and clock in for his shift.

By the time we wrapped up the investigation, there was more than enough video and license plate data to confirm the thefts. The Volvo was entered into NCIC, and Metro police was notified of his address for follow-up. One auto theft charge had already been filed, more were coming.

He thought he was clever, using his employee access like a skeleton key. But once the cameras started rolling, his "inside job" was about as subtle as driving a stolen BMW past the front door. This guy did it while still on the payroll, walking back into work like nothing had happened. I know there can be a lot of frustration with rental car companies, but they put a lot of policies in place to help prevent this type of activity. They lose millions in cars every year because of fraud and theft, from the inside and out.

THE MIDNIGHT FILL-UPS

It started with a hunch from a manager. An airline maintenance company had its own fuel pumps behind the cargo building, reserved strictly for company vehicles. But the logs weren't adding up.

When the manager pulled the records, a strange pattern jumped out—back-to-back fill-ups of ten or eleven gallons, always about ten minutes apart. They were happening late at night or in the early morning hours, almost always on the same nights a particular employee was on shift.

The theory was simple: she was filling two five-gallon cans, carrying them out to the parking lot, and topping off her personal car with company fuel.

The logs alone might have been circumstantial, but her airport badge told the rest of the story. Back-to-back gate swipes from her airport-issued ID badge matched every suspicious fill-up—one to step out to the lot, and another ten minutes later to come back inside. It was clockwork.

January's records painted the clearest picture: two fill-ups on the 4th, the 11th, the 19th, and again on the 26th. Each one lined up with her schedule, each one with matching gate activity, each one siphoning off the company's dime.

It wasn't a complex operation. No elaborate fraud. Just a midnight gas run, repeated and again, until the paper trail told the entire story. What stuck with me was how something so small—ten gallons here, ten gallons there—was enough to cost someone their career. She didn't get caught by a sting or a camera, just by routine records that told the truth. Records that any reasonable person would know about, since you have to enter your employee number and a code to get the gas out of the pump. Maybe she didn't care? It was a reminder that in investigations, the simplest evidence can sometimes speak the loudest.

THE BATTERY BANDIT

During the cold winter months, airline maintenance inspects ground equipment more often to make sure it's in good shape for the winter cold. We received several reports from the patrol guys of stolen batteries from ground power units, air start units, and even semi-trucks. Thousands of dollars in batteries gone, and even worse, it's occurring on the terminal ramp in a restricted area. We picked up good surveillance of the suspect's vehicle, an unusual Pontiac Torrent SUV. There were few of those on the road, but we could not identify any suspects with that lead. A break came after a week when a maintenance worker had just recently checked a ground power unit and discovered its battery was missing. The window was small. He had checked it the day before, so we knew we could review video in the area and maybe get lucky, and we did. Overnight, a small pickup truck from an aircraft fueling company backed in next to the power unit. We backtracked the truck to the entry gate, where employees are required to swipe their airport ID badge to enter the ramp. Now we had him identified. We wanted to gather more evidence before interviewing him and found out his mom had a certain rare vehicle registered to her. The same-colored Pontiac Torrent that was seen during one of the thefts. I pulled him in for an interview and hit him hard, telling him we could seize his mom's SUV since it was used during the commission of a felony theft. I asked him if he really thought he was going to get away with it. He had a deer-in-the-headlights look and mumbled, "not really." I booked him into jail on multiple counts of theft and burglary. We didn't seize his mom's car. This was one of many cases where diligence and good investigative work paid off. When I have a lot of evidence of a crime against an identified suspect, the interviews will always start with questions where I already know the answer. I'll let the suspect dig a hole so deep that there's no way they're getting out of it when I finally get into the meat of the interrogation.

THE VENDING MACHINE CAPER

A high-end electronics retailer had a couple of vending machines inside the main terminal—the kind stocked with expensive electronics for travelers who suddenly realized they needed headphones, chargers, or a tablet before boarding. One day, an employee called us after finding repeated "forced open" alarms in the vending machines' internal system logs. Both units in the terminal showed the same alarms, and the inventory was short—by a lot. The employee gave us exact dates and times for each alarm, which made the video review a lot easier. One of the vending machines that was hit was right next to a door with a security camera aimed at it. We pulled the footage and were surprised to find the culprit wasn't an outsider. It was a skycap—someone who worked in the terminal every day—using a screwdriver to pry the machine's door open just enough to slide his hand in and pull out merchandise. He'd been doing it overnight, when no one was around and got several thousand dollars' worth of electronics in a very short time. Once the retailer confirmed they wanted to prosecute, we took out a felony warrant. We put a trace on his airport badge, and sure enough, not long after, it pinged. We took him into custody without incident. The kicker? A few months later, we caught his mother—also an airport employee—with a cell phone at their home a passenger had reported missing. The owner didn't want to prosecute, but mom's badge was revoked, and she lost her job. Apparently, theft had become a family activity. You expect thieves to come in from the outside, not for people who already have the privilege of working inside the airport to abuse it. Seeing both a son and his mother lose their jobs over theft was a reminder that sometimes the worst damage comes from the people already on the inside.

FIFTY-ONE DOLLARS AND A LOST CAREER

In 2017, a corporate security investigator contacted me from one of our airlines about a theft that had occurred inside their office area. Employees reported that a small charity jar—holding about fifty-one dollars in cash—had gone missing earlier that morning.

The office was under surveillance by cameras operated by the airline's corporate security office in Florida. Reviewing the footage, the investigator spotted the culprit: a cleaning employee. The video showed him enter the office, turn the lights off, and pocket the jar before casually pushing a trash cart toward the freight elevator.

I pulled the freight elevator footage myself. When the doors opened, the man's hands hovered awkwardly near his pockets. On the cart sat a trash bag that had come from the airline office. He tied it up tightly before exiting the elevator on the service level, heading straight for the compactors.

The investigator advised the airline didn't want to prosecute, but they did want to recover the missing $51 and, of course, deal with the employee. I responded to the airline office and spoke with the cleaning supervisor, instructing him to confiscate the employee's airport badge when he reported for work.

When the employee showed up later, I met him in the parking garage and asked him to sit in the front seat of my vehicle. He already knew what this was about. Embarrassed, he admitted to making a "stupid decision." He told me he had only taken the dollar bills from the jar, then tossed the jar into the trash bag before sending it down into the compactor. The money, he said, was spent on gas and food.

His story matched the video evidence. The airline declined to prosecute, but his career at the airport ended that day. Fifty-one dollars isn't much, but it was enough to cost him his badge, his job, and his future at the airport. Out of all the theft cases I worked, this was one of the clearest reminders that sometimes it's not the amount stolen that matters—it's the choice.

WHEN THE GATEKEEPER GOES ROGUE

In 2017, a rental car manager reached out to me about several vehicles that had gone missing from their inventory. After running the plates, about three of the vehicles popped up in our Long Term parking lot. Surveillance video showed different men behind the wheel of the rentals, slipping them into the lot as if it were their own private storage yard.

One vehicle in particular, a Toyota Avalon, stood out. It had been missing since June 2, but video showed it cruising into the Long Term lot on June 13, June 26, and again on June 28. Finally, on July 6, the Avalon turned back up in the rental garage like nothing had happened.

I gave the rental manager photos I had pulled from my airport video footage, and the driver of the Avalon wasn't a stranger—it was one of their own employees. When I sat down with him, he flatly denied ever having driven the vehicle. When I pushed back, pointing out I had him on camera not once but twice, his story shifted. He admitted he might have driven it "once," then backpedaled to say maybe more than once. Evasive answers were all I got.

This employee worked the exit gate in the rental garage, meaning he could wave cars out without raising suspicion. A position of trust, and he abused it. He swore he knew nothing about the other missing cars or the other men we'd seen driving them, but it was clear he wasn't telling the whole truth.

Digging further, I learned his driver's license had been revoked back in April. That made his "test drives" a crime on multiple levels. In the end, I took out two arrest warrants against him—one for driving on a revoked license, and one for joyriding. He was lucky; joyriding is a lesser offense than auto theft and a misdemeanor. If you haven't seen the trend yet, rental car companies deal with a lot of inside problems, and there's not one company that is immune from it. Some deal with it better than others, but in a very litigious society, they just want to terminate the employee and move on. There were quite a few cases throughout my career where these companies should have pursued criminal charges. It was getting worse when I retired.

BROKEN SYSTEM, BROKEN KIDS

Auto burglaries weren't common in our airport garages—too much foot traffic and too many cameras. But when they happened, the cameras usually made quick work of the case. One day, I received a call about several vehicles that had been rummaged through. When I started reviewing video footage in the area, I caught a juvenile wandering through the garage, methodically checking door handles. Every unlocked car was an open invitation—and disturbingly, he found a lot of them. Within an hour, he'd been inside over a dozen vehicles, helping himself to whatever he could grab. The twist? His mother worked at the airport. While she was inside renewing her airport badge, he was outside in the garage breaking into cars. When she came back and didn't see him in hers, she simply left—no calls to us that her son was missing, no concern. The cameras showed him using his phone to call her for a pickup later. And here's the kicker—he was wearing an ankle monitor the entire time. Pulling the data from the ankle monitor gave us a perfect timestamp trail that matched our video from the parking garage. Fortunately, no guns or high-value items were taken—just some spare change and a pair of headphones. Still, leaving your vehicle unlocked anywhere, even in a "safe" garage, is just asking for trouble. I charged him with multiple counts of burglary. His mother eventually lost her job at the airport, but it was obvious she had little interest in supervising him. Watching him on video that day, it was clear he had zero concern about consequences—a mindset we saw often in kids involved in burglary, auto theft, and even violent crimes. The court system didn't help much. For juveniles, it was often a revolving door—arrested one day, back out the next. I know the problems run deeper than law enforcement alone can fix, but after years of watching the same young offenders cycle through, it wore on the entire team. And it was never just one offense they were involved in.

THE PHONE, THE CASH, AND THE CLEANING LADY WHO WOULDN'T STAY QUIET

A simple lost-and-found call turned into one of those cases that shows how quickly poor decisions can derail a career.

An employee who worked at the airport's Information Center, emailed me about a phone that had been turned in under suspicious circumstances. An airline employee had brought it over, saying he'd found it. The phone had a case on it—and inside that case was not only a Southwest credit card belonging to a Southwest customer but also a crisp $50 bill. Or at least, it was supposed to be.

The moment the airline employee turned the phone in, a female cleaning employee named showed up, repeating "fifty dollars, fifty dollars," and telling airport customer service to check the airline employee's pockets. Through her supervisor's translation, the cleaning lady explained she'd been the one to actually find the phone and had handed it to the Southwest employee because of the Southwest credit card inside. She said she then saw him try to stash the phone in a drawer behind the Southwest counter—and slip the $50 cash into his pocket. When she confronted him, he got flustered and finally walked it down to the Information Center, but by then the cash was gone.

I pulled the video and it told the story frame by frame. At 7:49pm, the cleaning lady hands the airline employee the phone. Thirteen seconds later, he's digging into the phone case. A few seconds after that, sliding his right hand into his pocket after opening that drawer. And less than three minutes after the cleaning lady first gave him the phone, he's handing it off to the employees at the information desk—minus the cash.

I identified the airline employee, and I had dealt with him before. I interviewed him privately behind the ticket counter. When I asked why he took the money, he didn't even bother with a cover story—just said, "I needed gas money."

He still had the $50 on him, which I confiscated. I explained that the passenger didn't want to press charges, but his airport badge had to go, and his future with the airline was effectively over. Airline management collected his credentials and keys, and I mailed the recovered cash back to the victim. A three-minute lapse in judgment cost the employee his job and his access to the airport. The cleaning lady had every reason to stay quiet—but instead, she told the truth and kept pressing until someone listened. On the other side was an airline employee who threw away a good job for fifty dollars. That contrast always stayed with me: one person's integrity shining at the same moment another's completely collapsed.

61 WIVES AND 81 KIDS

In 2016, what started as a routine drug investigation opened the door to one of the more bizarre theft cases I'd seen. We were tracking a suspect believed to be flying one of the airlines out of our airport to pick up controlled substances. Nothing unusual about that part—it happens often enough. But when I dug into his travel, I realized he wasn't even paying for the tickets. He was flying on someone else's employee flight benefits.

The airline employee in question had been out on medical leave since June of that year, but his travel records told a different story. A subpoena to corporate security confirmed it: flights were being booked in his name for multiple "spouses" and "dependents." According to company policy, flight benefits cover the employee, their actual spouse (or designated companion), and children—either dependent minors, students under 23, or nondependent children still under 23. Pretty straightforward.

But this guy? He was listing multiple men and women as his "spouse" at the same time and assigning strangers as his "children." During just one year, he had 61 different spouses and 81 different dependents flying for free under his benefits. Corporate estimated the airline lost nearly $72,000 in revenue from his antics.

And he wasn't alone. A second employee was caught doing the same thing, padding his account with 110 fake dependents in one year for another $50,000 in losses. Together, they'd turned the airline's family benefit program into a black-market travel agency.

Both employees eventually showed up at the airport police station voluntarily. One admitted outright that he'd booked the flights and was being paid $150–$250 per ticket to list strangers as his relatives. The other tried to shift the blame, saying his brother-in-law had his login and was the one making the fraudulent reservations. When we interviewed the brother-in-law, he admitted as much. He told us he'd been running names through the system for friends, old classmates, and sometimes people he didn't even know. He knew it was wrong—he just didn't realize how much money it added up to until the airline showed him the numbers. In the end, all three—two employees and the brother-in-law—were charged with felony theft. For me, the case was a reminder that theft doesn't always involve cash being pulled from a register or cars being driven off a lot. Sometimes it's as simple as turning a perk into a criminal enterprise.

THE CIRCUIT TRACER TRAIL

The airport's primary electrical contractor came to my office after one of his crews reported missing equipment. A circuit tracer—a tool electricians depend on—had vanished from a truck parked in the airport garage. The employee swore he always stored it in the same side compartment, and when it disappeared, suspicion immediately fell on a contract worker who'd done something unusual that day: stayed behind while the rest of the crew went to lunch.

We pulled the video. Sure enough, there he was on camera—walking up to the truck, opening the exact compartment, and rooting around where the tracer was supposed to be.

Digging further, we learned the man was already on probation for theft. That made things easier. A quick pawn database check showed multiple recent transactions tied to him and his mother. The list included—no surprise—the "Ideal" brand circuit tracers, the very tools missing from the trucks. He had also pawned several other electrical tools that ended up being stolen from the same trucks.

By that afternoon, we were standing inside a pawnshop with the company owner and his employee, staring at their stolen tools on the shelf. From there, we followed the trail to a second shop, where the other tracer turned up. The evidence couldn't have been clearer.

Later that night, Metro officers and I served the warrant. Our thief's short side hustle was over. He hadn't just stolen tools; he'd left a circuit-traced path right back to himself.

The company owner stood shoulder to shoulder with me as we walked into those pawn shops, and he saw for himself that his trust in our process was paying off. He told me later he'd never had an agency follow through the way we did. That meant something—not just for him, but for me and my team. Cases like this reminded me that good police work isn't just about making an arrest; it's about building trust with the people who keep the airport running every day.

CASHIER'S CUT: PARKING BOOTH EMBEZZLEMENT

In 2016, the airport parking lot manager called me about a parking cashier who wasn't just making change—she was making money disappear.

They suspected one of their cashiers of stealing cash and asked me to review video footage from the booths. I went back a few weeks on video, and it didn't take long before I saw exactly what management was worried about. On multiple occasions, I observed the cashier in question, as well as two other female cashiers, stuffing cash and receipts into purses and pockets like it was part of the job.

Management identified the other two women. The younger one was the rookie, only a month on the job, while the older one had been around for eight months and was the most frequent hand in the till. Management pulled transaction records, and the receipts missing during the senior employee's shifts added up to more than $1,600, a felony.

When the original employee was confronted, she folded quickly. She admitted that the senior female taught her how the scheme worked: if a valet customer paid cash, she would give the senior employee the receipt, who would then dispose of it and slip her some cash back out of the register. The system made it look like the transaction never happened, and the registers never came up short.

The senior employee didn't even bother trying to deny it. She admitted right away that she'd been pocketing cash, though she downplayed her take, claiming she never made more than $300 over her entire eight months on the job. The numbers told a different story.

Junior employee got off with a misdemeanor citation for theft under $500, but senior wasn't as lucky. With the video evidence and the large amount involved, she was taken into custody and booked on a felony.

It was a simple reminder that no matter how small the booth or the job might seem, theft at the airport always shows up on camera. It also illustrates how quickly bad habits can spread. One dishonest employee trained the next, and soon theft had become routine—almost like it was part of the job. They knew a camera was looking down right over their heads, but took the chance anyway.

THE RESTAURANT MANAGER WHO COOKED THE BOOKS

In 2023, I spoke with an executive of a company that managed several restaurants that were in the airport. She spoke about a problem she didn't want to believe—one of her own managers was stealing from the company. The red flags had started showing up around September, when they noticed that their night deposits from one of their restaurants weren't adding up. The same name kept coming up with the missing cash: the restaurant manager.

By the time we spoke, the losses were already over $14,000. She handed me video footage showing the manager in the back office with several deposit bags laid out on a table. The footage was damning: he was pulling bills from one bag, stuffing them into others, clearly trying to paper over earlier shortages.

She confronted the manager face-to-face. She asked him about the missing deposits and the video showing his sleight of hand. He didn't admit it, but he didn't deny it either—he just sat there, cornered, and said nothing.

She wanted prosecution. As I dug deeper, I learned something that made the $14,000 theft look like small change. This manager was already under investigation in a state out west for stealing more than $200,000 from a large restaurant chain during his time as a manager there. The jurisdictional agency confirmed they had an open case, but it hadn't even been assigned to a detective yet. So his background was still clear when he was hired at the airport.

For us, the evidence was clear. A direct presentment was prepared for the District Attorney's office charging the manager with theft over $10,000. This wasn't an employee skimming a few bucks from a register—this was a manager trusted with the books, stealing from his own company while smiling across the counter. And worse, it wasn't his first time. The gap between what he'd already done out west and what he was able to do here showed me how easy it was for repeat offenders to slip through the cracks. Sometimes the most dangerous thieves aren't the ones breaking in from the outside—they're the ones already sitting in the manager's chair.

THE JOB INTERVIEW THAT GAVE HIM AWAY

In 2017, I got an email from one of the car rental managers about a missing SUV. A black Nissan had dropped off the radar. According to their records, it was last returned a month before, but hadn't been seen since.

I started by running the license plate through our parking system, and sure enough, there was a hit: the Nissan had entered one of the long-term lots in mid-June. Video showed a young male in a yellow-and-red striped shirt behind the wheel. Another hit came a month later in mid-July, when the Nissan exited the same lot. But here's where it got interesting—the ticket used to exit didn't belong to the Nissan at all. It belonged to another vehicle, an orange Chevrolet, with a license plate number registered to RG.

I pulled video from the lot entrance, and it confirmed RG was behind the wheel of that Chevy. Now we had two possible suspects circling this case.

A week later, while digging further, I learned RG had recently applied for a job with one of the airlines. I contacted their HR staff and asked for the interview list from July 14—the same day the black Nissan slipped out of the lot. One name stood out: MJ. Running his information through a local law enforcement database gave me my confirmation. His booking photo matched the driver of the Nissan caught on video.

To tighten the case, I checked further. Sure enough, metro police had already pulled MJ over on a few days before he entered one of the airport parking lots while he was driving the missing black Nissan That traffic stop sealed it. I swore out warrants against him for theft over $10,000 and driving on a suspended license.

It started as just another missing rental car. But by following the trail through parking lot records, security video, and even a job interview, the entire scheme unraveled. MJ didn't just lose his shot at a new career—he picked up felony theft charges instead.

This case reminded me of another time when a job application gave a suspect away. We were dispatched to a commercial office building near the airport for a strong-armed robbery. A woman reported that a man had approached her in the parking lot, snatched her purse, and fled. We didn't catch him on scene, but when we pulled the building's security footage, there he was—walking out just minutes before the robbery, fresh off filling out an application for a janitorial job.

Sometimes, you don't need fingerprints or DNA to solve a crime. All you need is a resume.

GAS AND GAMESTOP

I received a call from an airline supervisor on the terminal ramp—a ramp employee said his debit card had been stolen from his locker. A quick check of the account showed charges at a gas station a few miles south of the airport, plus another at a GameStop. I headed to the GameStop first. They had a solid camera system and were willing to pull the footage. The video wasn't crystal clear, but it didn't have to be—we recognized the culprit right away. He was another ramp worker. The footage even showed him helping a couple of buddies fill their gas tanks on the victim's card before heading into the store. Two days later, we walked into the airline's employee area and took him into custody—in full view of his coworkers. Arrests like that serve two purposes: they make an impression on the suspect, and they send a message to anyone else thinking about doing the same thing. I've said it a hundred times—even a $5 purchase on someone else's credit or debit card is identity theft, and it is a felony in most states. Those card numbers are unique to the person they're issued to. The "big" theft cases aren't about dollar amounts—they're about trust broken, and the example you set when you put the cuffs on in front of everyone else.

THE DAY LABOR DILEMMA

Over the years, I worked a lot of cases involving rental car companies—fraud, auto theft, even the occasional drug overdose. But one of the recurring issues came from the same source: day laborers. The big rental brands often brought in temporary workers to wash and fuel cars, and while the convenience was obvious, the background checks were... questionable. One case started with a call from a rental company security rep. Several cars had gone missing, and he suspected one of their temp workers—a young woman. He gave me the license plates, and I ran them through our LPR cameras at the rental garage exit. The pattern jumped out immediately: the same woman was leaving in the middle of her shift, behind the wheel of brand-new rental cars, and driving them away from the airport. Video confirmed it, and by the time we pulled her in for an interview, we'd counted five cars. She already had prior auto theft charges on her record, and this wasn't a complicated operation—she admitted she'd been selling the cars on the street for a couple hundred dollars each. The exit booth attendants never questioned her. She was wearing a rental company uniform, so they assumed she had a reason to take the cars out. She didn't. I charged her with multiple counts of auto theft, and patrol took her to jail. The company eventually recovered the vehicles. That case was a turning point. The rental company and our detective team started vetting these workers more closely. Whenever they scheduled a "maintenance run"—when six to eight vehicles would leave the garage together for service—we'd check the drivers' licenses on the spot. It was quick, didn't slow down operations, and it gave us valuable information.

Several of those licenses turned out to be suspended, and a few of the drivers had outstanding warrants. It forced the labor companies to finally tighten up their background checks before sending temp workers to drive away cars worth tens of thousands of dollars. It was a good partnership between the police department and the rental car company that ended well for both. One of the best things you can gain as a detective is the networking with other law enforcement agencies and private partners.

BAGS, SCAMS, AND STICKY FINGERS

THE DUTY-FREE COUNSELOR

It was the middle of the summer, and flights were full. The general manager over the retail shops in the terminal called my office on Monday about a tremendous loss from their stores over the weekend. The manager observed the same individual on their video system in several of the airport shops and saw him shoplifting. I reviewed our video as well and backtracked his movements throughout the airport terminal. The suspect was male, probably in his late 40s, early 50s, and I was amazed at the amount of merchandise he took from all the shops. After reviewing a ton of video, I figured out he flew in on United Airlines on Friday and flew back out on Sunday. After sending a subpoena to the airline, I finally had a name. What I learned next was crazy. The total loss from all the retail shops was over $13k. The suspect? a guidance counselor at a high school in Nevada. I took out an arrest warrant for felony theft and contacted the school. The principal told me that this counselor was known among the school staff as the "duty-free guy," because he always had merchandise to sell that he claimed he picked up from the airport duty-free stores. His hobbies on the school webpage included traveling around the country to visit universities. According to the principal, this guy had over a million sky miles with United Airlines. Turns out, he was also a career thief and used the airlines to facilitate his trade. After the warrant was issued, the counselor came to court and wrote a $13k check to the retailer. The courts put him on probation, and he lost his job with the school. After watching the video, I learned he had sewn extra-large pockets in a jacket he carried. He would load the merchandise into those pockets and then leave the stores. And when I say load, he would literally empty entire pegs of goods at one time. He would then empty the loot from those hidden pockets into a large carry-on bag at a nearby gate and repeat the process. By day, he was guiding kids at school; by night, he was looting airports across the country. I could only imagine how many thefts he had pulled off before he landed in my airport. But here at least, his run was over.

THE JAGUAR LUGGAGE THIEF

For a couple years, I worked hard to identify a bag thief, and that eventually paid off. She was in her early to mid-50s and drove a convertible Jaguar. This didn't fit a typical profile of someone who came into the terminal on at least three occasions and stole luggage off the belt. I never understood luggage theft; you are literally playing Russian roulette with what you get out of the bag, and often, it's just worn clothes. This woman was testing my patience because she was so sporadic. She would only do it if she was at the terminal dropping someone off or picking someone up. At the time, we had a crappy video system and no LPR cameras, so I could never get her identified. Finally, we received a report of a missing bag off the belt, and it was indeed her. She had an older lady with her in a wheelchair, and we were able to backtrack this woman picking the older lady up from the Southwest gate. A subpoena was sent to Southwest, and there were only two wheelchair passengers on the plane. The lady in the wheelchair ended up being the suspect's mother, and we learned she was flying back out the next week. My team and I set up on the day of the flight and, sure enough, the suspect pulls up to the terminal, drops her mother off with a skycap for help, and then pulls around and parks in the garage. I was so stoked when I saw do this because I knew she was coming in. We got eyes on her as soon as she walked into the terminal. She walked into the baggage claim area, took two bags, and proceeds right out the door. We let her get to the garage and start to load the bags into her trunk before we approached her, identified ourselves as police officers, and took her into custody. Inside her purse was a loaded .357 revolver. We charged her with felony theft and with carrying a loaded weapon into the airport. She tried to give us a Robin Hood story about how she was taking the clothes from the stolen luggage and giving them to employees where she worked who were less fortunate than her. She was booked into jail on the charges, and at her court appearance, she wrote a check to reimburse several airlines that had already paid out the victims for the loss involving the luggage she had stolen.

For years, she had slipped through cracks in our weak technology, stealing sporadically enough to avoid a pattern. But patience and persistence paid off. She turned out to be just another thief with a gun in her purse—and she finally ran out of luck at our airport.

THE PURPLE POLKA-DOT BUST

Another luggage theft that comes to mind involves a supervisory nurse from a hospital in the Midwest. I was following up on a report about a bag that went missing from the belt. It belonged to a little girl and was purple with polka dots. I loved cases like these because the bag stood out. After working many years in investigations, if I were to give any advice to travelers, it is to make your bags stand out. 80-90% of bags are solid blue or solid black. If yours comes up missing, it's almost impossible to identify it if it looks like everyone else's. In this case, the polka dots burned the suspect. Ironically, she had flown in on the same flight as the victim. The victim and her mother were a little late getting to baggage claim because they had to stop at the restroom. When they got to there, the bag was nowhere to be found. After reviewing video footage, I located the female suspect taking the bag and entering a taxi. I sent subpoena records and learned that the taxi had taken her to a nice hotel south of town. Her employer had paid for the hotel room. My next subpoena went to the employer, and I met with one of their chief attorneys in a large commercial building near town. The attorney explained to me that the employee in question was a nurse supervisor at one of the hospitals that the company owned. You could tell it they were taking it seriously from the atmosphere. The attorney provided me with all the employee's information as well as where she worked. I attempted to contact the suspect several times, but she never returned my calls. I called the director of human resources at the hospital and explained the situation. That one of their supervisors had an outstanding felony warrant, was avoiding my calls, and needed to come and book herself on the warrant. An hour later, the nurse called me from the human resources office, and I explained the outstanding warrant against her. She lost her job that day and learned that what was in the bag she stole was not worth the consequences. I never got the polka dot bag back, but the nurse had to pay out around $1,000 as part of her plea agreement in court. A nurse trusted to supervise others, undone by stealing a child's suitcase. All that responsibility, all that trust—thrown away for a bag that turned out not to be worth it.

THE THANKSGIVING BAGGAGE CREW

Holidays always brought a different kind of chaos to the airport. The lines were longer, the flights were packed, and baggage claim was full of stressed families trying to get where they needed to be. And it also meant opportunity for thieves who knew when the distractions would be at their peak.

Over Thanksgiving weekend, reports started coming in about missing luggage. Not just one bag, but several. Reviewing video, it quickly became clear this wasn't a lone thief working the carousel. It was a crew. They blended in like any other family, hanging around the baggage belts until they spotted a chance. Then one person would grab a bag and hand it off to another, who walked it out the door.

We worked through hours of footage until we had them identified, even catching them on camera coordinating their moves. Subpoenas tied them all to the same vehicle, a silver Lexus ES sedan. It was a rash on the metro police's system, committing thefts all over the south end of town. This crew was hooked on pills.

Eventually, the crew was charged. None of the luggage was recovered, but what struck me most about this case wasn't just the thefts—it was the timing. While families were traveling to be with loved ones, while people were carrying gifts and clothes for a holiday week, these thieves were out looking for opportunities.

Thanksgiving is supposed to be about gratitude. Instead, these suspects saw it as a shopping spree in baggage claim. And for them, it ended with handcuffs and felony charges instead of a holiday.

THE BACKPACK FULL OF KEYS

What started as a simple rental car theft case ended up uncovering a far bigger problem—one hiding in plain sight in the employee break room.

We were arresting a rental employee for stealing a car. As he was heading to jail, we asked where his belongings were, and he said they were in a blue backpack in the breakroom. The rental manager went to grab it, but instead of finding the suspect's things, he opened a bag stuffed with dozens of key fobs. Not just any keys—these were high-dollar fobs, the kind that can cost several hundred dollars each to replace depending on the make of the vehicle.

The twist? The bag didn't belong to the employee going to jail. It belonged to someone else.

We brought that second employee in for questioning, and the story spilled out. He had been attending a technical school when a classmate bragged to him about an easy side hustle: steal key fobs from the rental car company, then sell them online for quick cash. The classmate claimed it was fast money, and apparently, he wasn't wrong. The student applied for a job at the airport rental counter, and once he had access, he started funneling the extra fobs off the vehicle key chains and into the black market.

I traced the online buyer, issued a subpoena, and sure enough, the company sent back receipts showing every single fob he'd sold. The numbers were staggering. The cost to replace those keys far outweighed what he was getting for them, but it added up fast. By the end of the case, we had him indicted on theft over $60,000.

All from a blue backpack that wasn't supposed to be his.

Family Ties and a Stolen iPhone

In August of 2015, I found myself standing in a Sam's Club parking lot, face-to-face with a man named Eric. He had arranged to meet me there to return a stolen iPhone. Eric claimed he'd bought it for $350 off Craigslist from some guy in a neighboring city. When I asked for his ID, he handed me his driver's license.

As I talked with him, the pieces connected. During my earlier digging, I had learned that one of the rental car shuttlers, a man named Damion, might be tied to the theft. I asked Eric if he knew Damion. His answer was short and telling: "He's my uncle."

That was enough to take me back to the airport's rental car facility, where I tracked Damion down. At first, he flat-out denied taking the phone. But after a little pressure, his story changed. He admitted he took it—though he insisted he "just found it" by the car wash area.

Damion's confession put me in the awkward spot of balancing cooperation with accountability. I told him the truth: it was up to the victim if charges would be pursued. Then, I gave him a ride to his car at the maintenance lot. He didn't seem all that concerned as he drove off airport property.

I called the victim, a woman named Linda, and let her know her phone had been recovered. She was relieved but cautious. She wanted to return the phone to AT&T and figure out what losses she might have suffered before deciding whether to press charges.

Finally, I notified the car rental security manager. Another employee theft investigation, this time tucked away in the shuffle of family ties and a supposedly "found" phone. This employee was risking his job and reputation over a phone, and we also had a nephew willing to cover for his uncle. It was a reminder that in airport policing, theft wasn't always about strangers in the terminal. Sometimes, it came down to people who worked side by side, and the family loyalty that blurred the lines between right and wrong.

. . .

The Maintenance Lot Thief Who Couldn't Stay Away

By the time my email pinged that October afternoon in 2017, the name attached to the case felt like an old acquaintance. The rental car company had reported that one of their vehicles, a white Ford Expedition, had turned up hundreds of miles away. It had supposedly been parked at the car rental maintenance lot for a routine oil change, yet somehow ended up being towed after the highway patrol pulled someone over in it.

That someone was T___ B___.

The name hit me instantly. I had arrested TB almost two years earlier, back when he was working maintenance for the same car rental company at the same maintenance lot. Back then he was caught sitting in a stolen Jeep Cherokee like it was just another work truck. Apparently, he hadn't learned much since.

This time, TB didn't even bother with much of a cover. He took the Expedition, drove it until he got caught, and left the rental company scratching their heads wondering how one of their vehicles wandered off the lot unnoticed. I called the rental car manager and gave her the news: TB was at it again.

There were still whispers of other cars gone missing from that maintenance lot, and I had no doubt he knew more than he was saying. For me, it was déjà vu—just another reminder that, at the airport, some thieves circle back like planes in a holding pattern, unable to resist returning to the scene of their last arrest.

THE VANISHED AMAZON PALLET

In 2017, I was contacted by the owner of a contract delivery company for Amazon, who believed one of his employees had stolen a large shipment of goods. Amazon had a distribution facility at the airport, so it fell in my lap. It was one of those layered operations where Amazon contracts to PR, PR contracts to DSA, and DSA contracts drivers from companies like his. The setup was already complicated, and this case didn't make it any easier.

In December, a driver left the Amazon facility with two pallets of products headed for a post office in a nearby city. Before leaving, there had been an altercation with Amazon staff. Amazon officials told the owner that they didn't want that driver returning to the facility. Whether he got the news before leaving or while out on his route, the timing turned out to be suspicious.

When the delivery route was complete, one post office never received its pallet. The driver, however, had scanned it into his app as though it had been delivered. That system is supposed to track a driver's location and confirm drop-offs, but in this case, it only confirmed that the package vanished somewhere between "picked up" and "supposedly delivered."

I asked the owner to send me the tracking data and inventory list, then executed a search warrant on the driver's apartment. Nothing. Not a single Amazon package turned up. The driver wasn't talking, and the trail went cold.

Amazon calculated the loss at over $10,000. Under the contract, the delivery company was on the hook to reimburse it. When I asked if he wanted to prosecute, the owner shrugged it off. No charges, no follow-up. To him, it was just the cost of doing business.

For me, it was weeks of investigation that ended in a dead end—a reminder that sometimes the people with the biggest losses would rather absorb them quietly than drag the problem into court.

THE BIKINI BAIT PHONE

A few years back, we had a nagging problem—skycaps and cleaning employees "finding" electronics and wallets in the terminal and somehow forgetting to turn them in to lost and found. I needed to send a simple message without a pile of court cases.

Many people know about the "bait cars" on TV that trap would-be auto thieves. In this case, enter the "bait phone." It was a nice Samsung in a case, but with some extra surprises. I could set it down anywhere in the terminal, activate it, and the moment someone picked it up, it would quietly start taking random pictures and sending me and my team real-time GPS tracking. The lock screen? A woman in a flashy bathing suit—irresistible to the curious. On my very first run, a skycap took the bait. He picked up the phone, boarded the employee shuttle to the parking lot, and started swiping through it. The phone was busy snapping photos of him the whole time. Once I saw he was headed for the employee parking lot, I called patrol to intercept him before he could leave. I took his airport badge and told him he wasn't getting it back. No charges— but without that badge, he wasn't working at the airport anymore. I ran the sting for a couple months. It was fun, effective, and word spread fast. Now, every new hire hears the same warning: if it's not yours, don't touch it. I know most people who leave something behind at the airport feel it's a lost cause to try to recover it, and it probably is at some airports. We followed up on every lost-property report at my airport. It was not a part of the job the detectives were crazy about, because it was very time consuming and if there wasn't evidence that it was stolen, then they didn't feel that the task should fall on them. When you work that job for long enough, you understand that finding a small item for someone, especially if it held sentimental value, made more of a lasting effect than most other cases you ever worked.

THE SECURITY VEST HEIST

Rental car thefts at the airport usually fell into two categories: sloppy joyriders or polished pros. This one landed squarely in the second.

It started with a BMW X7, rented with a Kentucky driver's license that looked legitimate enough on the surface. But when the vehicle wasn't returned, it didn't take long to discover that the man who rented it wasn't the man on the license.

As I dug deeper, the picture got bigger. The same suspect had also slipped out of the garage in a brand-new GMC Yukon, this time wearing a black hoodie, reflective vest, and a ball cap with "SECURITY" plastered across the front. The exit gate employee waved him through without question—after all, he looked like he belonged there.

Managers from the rental companies tried to follow the Yukon as it left the airport. They trailed it to a McDonald's down the road, but lost the suspect when he abandoned the SUV and climbed into a white Dodge Ram. That truck, it turned out, was also a rental—missing from the Atlanta airport.

At the same McDonald's parking lot, another man was spotted snapping photos of a dark BMW SUV, likely the very one rented under the fake license. From experience, I knew what that meant. Pictures get sent to "shops" that specialize in flipping stolen cars—removing VIN plates, swapping tags, and making the vehicles disappear into the underground market.

Sure enough, license plate readers soon picked up the BMW in the Atlanta area, confirming that the entire operation tied back to a theft crew working out of Georgia. The BMW was entered into NCIC as stolen, another case file in a string of thefts pulled off by suspects who knew how to exploit uniforms, blind spots, and just enough confidence to drive off the lot. This guy fooled several rental car companies simply by wearing a reflective vest and clothes with the word "SECURITY." We caught a break when he attempted to rent a vehicle wearing that outfit at one of the newer rental car counters. Their equipment took pictures of the renter at the time of the rental as well as made color copies of the ID used. Through some newer technology we had gained and some investigative work, we identified him. The next time he came to the airport, he was stopped, but only after getting into a foot pursuit. The officers grabbed him by his long dreads as he tried to run. He faced close to a dozen felony charges, all stemming from stolen rental cars and fraud.

It wasn't the first time I dealt with someone posing as an employee to get a rental car out of the garage. We had several cases where actual temp workers just pulled up to the gate and were let out, because they were, in fact, working at the airport. This guy in particular was bold, and he wore the same clothes with security stamped all over it to get some very nice vehicles. He had a pretty lengthy criminal history in Georgia. Just as with most criminals I've dealt with in the past, he got greedy. That was a common trend with these guys. They'd get a car or two, make some decent money, and then it was like Vegas. They either couldn't stop or didn't want to, and it always caught up to them.

LIKE MOTHER, LIKE DAUGHTER

In 2021, a Southwest supervisor called me about a suspicious bag theft off one of their belts in baggage claim. A passenger named Christina had reported her pink hard-sided bag missing after a flight in from Florida.

Southwest knew the bag in question had been scanned off the airplane and placed on the belt, just like it was supposed to be. I found a similar pink bag and emailed Christina a photo. She replied that it looked close—but hers had gray wheels, a gray zipper, and a matching handle. This struck me as odd, because it was the only pink, hard-sided bag on the belt, and it went right by her. She didn't look twice at it.

I went back through the cameras and spotted a white female entering baggage claim from outside the terminal. She wore a gray shirt, blue scrub-style pants, and had a large tattoo down her left arm—and was clearly walking out with the same pink hard-sided bag that I had seen on the belt. Moments earlier, I had seen this girl getting out of a silver Nissan Altima.

I ran the plate through our LPR system. The registered owner? None other than Christina's daughter. Both mother and daughter lived at the same address.

That alone was suspicious, but the story got better. A Southwest employee told me Christina had filed a lost bag claim with a different airline just a month earlier and had already been paid for it. Many of the airlines will pay up to $3,000 for a lost bag. I pulled video from June when she also flew in on Southwest and, sure enough, there she was hauling around the same pink bag—identical to the one her daughter had now "stolen." I also sent the Florida airport that Christina had flown in from all the flight information so they could check their cameras. They got the information on Christina's flight, and sent me a photo of her checking the same bag in at their ticket counter.

The scam was clear. I charged Christina with a felony for filing a false police report and told the airline not to pay her another dime for this bag.

Some people try to pull a fast one on the airlines. Christina took it a step further—roping in her own daughter and forgetting the cameras never stop rolling. It wasn't the first time she had done it, and I doubt it was the first time for her daughter either.

THE FIREFIGHTER FAKER

Baggage theft at the airport is rare, but it happens. I'd already had one case that took a while to solve, and then came another—different suspect, same kind of problem.

This guy was in his late thirties. After the first couple of thefts, we learned from reviewing video footage that he'd been arriving at the airport on a city bus. That made tracking him tricky—no car to plug into the LPR system, and no predictable schedule to catch him on.

One day he showed up in a city fire department uniform. At first glance, you might think he was legit. But something about him didn't sit right. Sure enough, he wasn't a firefighter at all. He had stolen the uniform—and a department-issued radio—right out of a fire truck while the real firefighters were inside a grocery store shopping.

He wasn't just targeting the airport either. He'd been hitting universities, businesses, and other buildings all over the city. We suspected he was homeless, moving constantly, which made him even harder to pin down.

The break came when another agency picked him up for an unrelated theft. We quickly took out multiple arrest warrants for the stolen luggage and served them while he was still in jail. He was also banned from ever setting foot on airport property again.

Most thieves try to blend in; he tried to stand out, wrapping himself in the authority of a firefighter's uniform. It was brazen, and it reminded me that in an airport, appearances can be deceiving. I haven't seen him since, so I hope he stays locked up for a while—but with the transient ones, you never really know where they'll pop up next.

BRA MONEY AND A BATHROOM BUST

While on patrol in the terminal, I was called to meet with a woman who had accidentally left her purse behind in the food court. As I was speaking with her, dispatchers notified me that a cleaner had found her purse in a nearby bathroom trash can. Everything was still inside—except for $500 in cash.

It didn't take long for us to find three young girls on video entering the bathroom with the victim's purse. I located them in another concourse and began asking questions. They all denied having anything to do with it.

I explained that based on the video alone, I had enough to charge each of them with felony theft. That changed their tone immediately.

Two of them immediately reached into their bras and started pulling out the money. The third was a little more stubborn, still sticking with her story that she did not know about the money. The other two gave her an earful, and she pulled out the remaining $100 bill from her bra.

The woman didn't want to press charges—she just wanted to catch her flight. She was thrilled to have her money returned. The girls were let go with a stern warning and an earful. I really wanted them to go to jail, but a lot of cases turned out this way. People who were not from here just wanted to get back home without dealing with jail and court. That was one of the biggest differences between an airport police department and a county or city agency. A majority of our victims of personal crimes were not locals, and they rarely wanted to return out of state to follow up on a criminal case, especially if it was on their own dime. It bothered me early in my investigative career, but I got used to it.

THE STUDENT WHO STUDIED CARS

In 2018, during the height of rental car fraud, a rental car manager flagged one of their own employees, a young man named A___ B___, after catching him behind the wheel of a white Chrysler 300 that he shouldn't have been driving. That was enough for them to end his employment, but it turned out the Chrysler was just the beginning.

When they dug into their inventory, they realized that three more vehicles—two Camaros and an Equinox—had quietly gone missing around the same time this employee was on the payroll. Suspicion fell on him immediately.

OnStar tracked one of the missing Camaros to the parking lot of a local technology college, where AB happened to be a student. The rental manager went to the college, spotted the Camaro, and started watching it until he spotted AB and another man walking out of the school. The second man went straight to the Camaro and tried to drive away, only to find himself blocked in by the rental car manager. When confronted, he claimed he was "just moving it for AB."

It didn't take long for the rest of the evidence to pile up. The school's director confirmed AB was seen speeding around campus in the Camaro. When the car was recovered, the keys were even attached to AB's apartment keys. Even the tinted windows were a giveaway—unauthorized modifications the rental company never allowed on their rentals.

The Camaros were recovered, but AB's "student project" in creative auto acquisition was over. What started as a job in the rental car garage ended with felony charges and a lesson learned the hard way: the company always keeps the receipts—and the GPS data. A couple of the rental car companies became more worried about lawsuits than getting police involved to recover their stolen cars. They started placing the burden on their managers, security reps, and contracted repo teams. I think it put many people in unnecessary danger, but this was late in my career, and it wasn't an issue I wanted to tackle.

NO FREE PARKING

It was a Sunday afternoon when airport operations radioed in about a silver BMW SUV at the parking lot exit booths. The driver was arguing with parking personnel about the $196 fee she owed. Before officers could get there, she decided the debate was over—she simply drove off without paying.

We spoke with the parking manager and booth attendant, who provided us with the vehicle's license plate number and even the suspect's state issued ID number. It wasn't even a valid driver's license, just an ID card. The name on it was Melissa.

We put together witness statements from the parking staff, then headed downtown to the Criminal Justice Center for warrants—one for theft of services, another for driving without a license. With paperwork in hand, we went to her listed address. Sure enough, the same silver BMW was sitting right in the driveway.

Metro officers met us there, and we knocked on the door. Melissa answered and didn't put up much of a fight.

In the end, she learned the hard way that driving past

the toll booth isn't a free pass—it's just a shortcut to a jail cell.

This happened more times than I could count. Parking fees are big money to an airport, but I shouldn't have to tell you that, because I assume many of you reading this book have paid to park at an airport. I think people believe that it's not worth the airport's time to skip out on $10, $15, $50 of parking. That may be the case at some airports, but not where I worked.

FALSE ALARMS, REAL CONSEQUENCES

THE DRUNKEN THREAT

Now and then, someone makes a threat against the airport and thinks it won't be taken seriously. This time, the caller was drunk—and not shy about it. Late at night, he told the dispatcher someone was going to "shoot up the airport."

He made my job easy. He called from his own cell phone—registered in his name, with a major carrier. Within a short time, I had his name and address. I headed south of town with a few officers and found our suspect: barely 21, living with his grandmother, fresh in from a night of clubbing.

It wasn't his only poor decision of the evening. He'd also tried calling the Russian embassy—thankfully, no one answered. We confiscated his phone and got a search warrant the next day. When we pulled his browser history, one search stood out: "punishment for bomb threat." I guess he wanted to see how much trouble he was in.

He got his answer—at least under state law. Because he had no prior criminal history, the court granted him judicial diversion. Sort of like probation, but if you stay out of trouble, the charge eventually gets dismissed. Word is, he later enlisted in the military.

What stuck with me about this case was the flip side of consequences. A careless threat could have changed his life forever—and almost did. But sometimes accountability doesn't just punish; it redirects. In his case, maybe the knock on the door that night was enough to push him toward a better path.

THE BEAR SPRAY BLOWUP

I got the call on a weekend—one of the airport concourses had been evacuated because of a strong chemical smell. Witnesses said it was like pepper spray, and they weren't far off. It only affected that one concourse, but it was strong enough to force everyone to evacuate to a different one. When that happens, the ripple effect is massive. Flights get delayed, thousands of travelers are affected, and it doesn't just stop at our airport—every connection down the line feels it. The good news was the smell came on suddenly in a very specific area, so we had a starting point. Reviewing the cameras, I spotted a cleaner emptying a trash can at the start of the concourse around the time the smell was first reported. He was fiddling with something in his hands, then—splat—a large mark appeared on the white wall behind him. He immediately tossed the item into his trash bin and pushed it down the concourse. We pulled him aside right away. There was a language barrier, but he explained it was some sort of small fire extinguisher-type device that "shot out." Oddly, it didn't bother him at all—no coughing, no tearing up. A search of the ramp dumpsters turned up nothing. But forty-five minutes before the cleaner showed up, the cameras caught another break: a man tossing the same device into that same trash can. He and a woman traveling with him were the last two to board a flight down that concourse before the evacuation. I subpoenaed the airline for their names and phone numbers. The phone number belonged to the woman, so I called. As soon as I explained who I was, she said, "This isn't about the bear spray, is it?" Bingo. She explained that she and her husband had been staying at a cabin in the mountains and were told to buy bear spray. After clearing the TSA checkpoint, her husband realized the screener had missed it in his bag. Not wanting to try his luck, he tossed it in the trash. Less than an hour later, the curious cleaner deployed it against the wall and then pushed it—still active—down the concourse in his trash bin. The woman insisted I call her husband directly because "if I tell him, he won't believe me." She'd already given him an earful about getting it past security. They were both retired military and good people. She was mortified to learn it had caused an evacuation. When I spoke to him, his story lined up perfectly with the video. They even sent me a picture of the exact product they'd bought. TSA later investigated the employee who'd hand-searched the bag and somehow missed the canister. It was purely accidental —but it caused one heck of an event. And it left everyone with a few lessons learned.

THE FRATERNITY FALLOUT

Some calls start strange and get stranger. This one came from a young man who phoned the airport police station asking to speak with a detective. I took the call, and he told me he was in a fraternity. Then came the accusation: he claimed a commercial airline pilot, who was an admin in the same fraternity, had threatened to "crash the airplane when he had the chance." I asked for the pilot's information, which he provided. He also claimed there were witnesses and other evidence to back up his story. I confirmed the pilot's identity and contacted the airline. Their response was quick—the pilot in question was currently on vacation with his family, traveling internationally as a passenger, not in the cockpit. Corporate representatives met with him when the plane landed, and he called me directly. His explanation painted a different picture. He was a director—maybe even a chapter president—of the same fraternity the caller belonged to. Recently, he had expelled the caller after catching him doing drugs at the fraternity and providing them to others. The pilot told me he'd be happy to discuss it further in person after returning from vacation. His background was impeccable—a solid military history, a clean, professional record. Meanwhile, I called the kid back and told him he needed to provide the witnesses' names and any evidence he'd promised. He never did. With no corroboration, I took out a felony warrant for filing a false police report. I didn't know what became of it until a few years later, when a prosecutor from another county called. The same kid had been arrested for auto theft in my county and later charged with providing drugs to a woman who overdosed and nearly died. He was convicted, and the prosecutor asked me to testify at his sentencing hearing about his false pilot threat. I testified and left, but later learned he had been sentenced to several years in prison. Apparently, he had a full-blown outburst in the courtroom and had to be restrained by deputies. Some people dig themselves into holes. This kid seemed determined to find the bottom. I had never seen someone so hellbent on refusing to take responsibility for anything.

THE DISGRUNTLED ATTENDANT

Several years ago, the sitting US president had flown into town, which meant extra security and a busier-than-usual day. VIPs at the airport weren't rare, but this day threw a curveball at us. We got word that a commercial aircraft was diverting to our airport because a written bomb threat had been found onboard. The plane landed and was directed to a secure staging area. These cases are resource-heavy—every single passenger is considered a suspect until proven otherwise. The passengers were escorted off the aircraft and into a secured area, leaving their bags behind. Then things escalated—one of our bomb dogs alerted to a carry-on bag. Federal agencies got a little more on edge, and our bomb squad moved in to X-ray the bag right there on the aircraft. The scan showed what looked like a laptop.

The bag's owner, a woman traveling for business, was located and interviewed. Her story lined up—she had no criminal history, and she begged us not to destroy her laptop. The decision was made to remove the bag. Our bomb techs suited up and carried it off the plane without incident. During the investigation, each passenger was instructed to write a sentence containing some of the same letters as the bomb note. That's how the focus shifted to an off-duty flight attendant. She'd written the note midflight out of spite toward the airline. Federal charges followed, and when she later tried to get them thrown out, the investigation and procedures held firm. After a further dive into the laptop bag, we figured out why the K9 had gone crazy—the woman had stored it in the trunk of her car, where her husband had recently been hauling fertilizer. The dog didn't smell explosives from a bomb... just the remnants of his last trip to the garden store. To top it all off, while all this was unfolding, another passenger came through the security checkpoint with an inert grenade in their bag. It was one of the busiest—and most chaotic—days our department had seen. Of note: The Secret Service used to park the motorcade near our station prior to the president's arrival. It gave us an opportunity to chat with them and see the cars up close. I have a picture of my oldest son and me standing outside of "the beast" when he was a toddler. That was a pretty cool moment during my career.

JEALOUSY IN THE AIR

Another threat case that sticks with me started over something petty—a girl upset that her best friend was paying too much attention to a new boyfriend. It began with a phoned-in bomb threat involving a flight to Tampa. The call came from a prepaid phone, so there wasn't much to trace. The female caller wasn't overly specific, just naming the airline and flight number. With no solid leads, the case stalled.

Then, Tampa Airport called. They'd had a similar threat involving a flight between our airport and theirs. We subpoenaed the records and found one common thread: a boy and girl who had flown on both trips. We went back through the original threat video and spotted them heading down the concourse together. Before security, another female had accompanied them. I shifted focus to her, and sure enough, she was on her phone minutes after leaving the couple—right around the time the threat was called in.

When I interviewed her, the motive was almost laughable if it hadn't been so disruptive. She admitted she didn't like the boyfriend because he was "interfering" with her friendship. She was from a rural part of the state and figured there was no way she'd be caught, but she was wrong.

I charged her with making the bomb threat—a felony. Her attempt to win back her friend's attention ended with attention no one wants—from law enforcement and the courts.

What stuck with me was how childish jealousy escalated into a federal-level investigation. To her, it was just a phone call. To us, it meant the possibility of locked-down flights, worried passengers, and a major disruption. It was a reminder that every threat has to be taken seriously, no matter how petty the motive seems.

REFLECTION

I hope you've enjoyed the stories I've shared in this book. There are others I could have told; some fascinating, some unbelievable, but certain details simply couldn't be included because of restricted information.

There's often a misconception that airport police officers are just glorified security guards. While our duties certainly included protecting the airport, our responsibilities went far beyond what most people see when they walk through the terminal doors. I think that's clear from what you've just read.

When I first started writing, I wasn't sure I'd have enough material to fill a full-length book. Turns out, I was wrong. As I sit here on the couch, watching my six-year-old smile at the TV, I'm reminded why I chose this career in the first place. I don't like bullies—and I'm thankful for parents who instilled empathy, integrity, and work ethic in me and my brothers. Those values shaped my desire to protect people who can't always protect themselves.

Lt. Col. Dave Grossman once described three kinds of

people: the sheep, who are peaceful and law-abiding; the wolves, who prey upon them; and the sheepdogs—those who protect the flock from the wolves. That analogy always resonated with me.

I was blessed to build our investigations division from the ground up and to work alongside skilled investigators from across Tennessee and beyond. If I have one regret, it's that toward the end of my career, I sometimes expected others to fight battles that were mine to handle. I should have known better. Still, I have no regrets about what my team accomplished. Together, we built one of the most respected investigative divisions in Middle Tennessee.

Eventually, it stopped being fun to go to work—and that's when I knew it was time to move on. I loved my job, and I was damn good at it, but it never defined who I was. I treated everyone the way I wanted to be treated, badge or no badge, and I believe that's a big part of why I found so much success in my career.

You never really know what someone else is going through, and I hope more people remember that—especially in today's world.

Stay safe, stay humble, and always pursue your dreams.

www.ingramcontent.com/pod-product-compliance
Lightning Source LLC
Chambersburg PA
CBHW060509030426
42337CB00015B/1815